Reading Research into the Year 2000

Reading Research into the Year 2000

Edited by

Anne P. Sweet
Judith I. Anderson
U.S. Department of Education

1993

LAWRENCE ERLBAUM ASSOCIATES, PUBLISHERS
Hillsdale, New Jersey   Hove and London

No official support or endorsement by the U.S. Department of Education is intended or should be inferred.

Lawrence Erlbaum Associates, Inc., Publishers
365 Broadway
Hillsdale, New Jersey 07642

Library of Congress Cataloging-in-Publication Data

Reading Research into the Year 2000 / edited by Anne P. Sweet and
   Judith I. Anderson
         p.   cm.
   Includes bibliographical referencecs and index.
   ISBN 0-8058-1305-5
   1. Reading—Research.   I. Sweet, Anne P.   II. Anderson, Judith I.
LB1050.6.R43   1993
428.4'072—dc20   92-41183
                                                       CIP

Books published by Lawrence Erlbaum Associates are printed on acid-free paper, and their bindings are chosen for strength and durability.

Printed in the United States of America
10 9 8 7 6 5 4 3 2 1

To David and Timothy

Table of Contents

Foreword

Milton Goldberg, Executive Director
National Education Commission on Time and Learning

Reading Research into the Year 2000 reflects the important work that has taken place, is now underway, and has yet to occur in the reading research discipline. Through the years, research on reading has made enormous contributions to helping us understand how students learn to read and how teachers can best instruct them. In *Research and Education Reform,*[1] the Committee on the Federal Role in Education Research of the National Academy of Science highlighted reading research as an area of work supported by the federal government that has substantially expanded our knowledge about the cognitive aspects of learning to read and has contributed to the development of innovative programs such as Reciprocal Teaching, Reading Recovery, and Success for All. Reading research continues to add to our fundamental understandings in significant ways, seeking to add more pieces to the puzzle/solution—for example, determining how students learn content in other school subjects through reading and what strategies teachers can use to help their students do this more effectively.

The contents of this book took shape during the time I was director of the Office of Research at the Office for Educational Research and Improvement (OERI). These contents portray the dynamic process that OERI engages in to plan a cutting-edge research agenda and set it into motion. It was written to inform a wide-reading public—those who benefit directly or indirectly from reading research findings, those who make research applications, and those who conduct the research. The contributors of this publication look forward to a dialogue with all those persons who have an

---

[1]Committee on the Federal Role in Education Research (1992). Research and the improvement of education. In R. C. Atkinson & G. B. Jackson (Eds.), *Research and education reform* (pp. 19–53). Washington, DC: National Academy Press.

interest in the literacy of our citizenry and the reading abilities of students in our nation's schools. We look forward to working with all those persons who will carry out the research and those who will disseminate the findings to those who will use them. Finally, we look forward to following the success of those who will (and do) implement research-based instructional practices in classrooms across the country.

Introduction

Anne P. Sweet
Judith I. Anderson
U.S. Department of Education

Why this book? What was our purpose in producing this documentation of the process for completing the National Reading Research Center? We believe that it is important to make the process public. Few people outside of the U.S. Department of Education are aware of the procedures undertaken to develop the mission statement and conduct a competition for a major research and development center. Traditionally, the number of people involved in the process has been small. Fewer than a handful of departmental staff are involved in the substantive and administrative support for the grant process. A handful of reviewers become part of the peer review process, and a handful of universities are part of the competition process. So, all in all, only a small number of people are "in the know" about the "ins and outs" of the process—and most of even this small number only know the particulars of the pieces in which they are involved.

The departmental staff know most about the research and development center grant planning process and the shaping of the center's mission: who was contacted, what the constraints were, how the funding was decided, how the field was surveyed. The peer reviewers know how the applications are evaluated and how recommendations are made for a funding decision. The applicants know how they decide what goes into the research agenda that they will submit for review. The winning applicant knows how to work with the government during negotiations to shape the final center activities. The unsuccessful applicants learn about the debriefing process. However, few have an overall picture.

Furthermore, many people—researchers as well as practitioners—are not involved in any phases of the process, let alone in a position to see the entire picture. Others are even further removed. Not only are they unaware of the processes involved in competing for and awarding a center, they are not even aware that the department funds educational research and development centers.

We believe that if more people are "in the know," they will be more likely to participate in the entire process—from generating research ideas to submitting applications—and that this greater participation is important. A reading research agenda that is being developed for the nation needs to be informed by the best thinking of the best minds. It needs to be informed not just by the research community, but by the broader community concerned with education: teachers, parents, administrators, and policy makers.

Up to now, there has been an exclusivity to the process of deciding what and whom to fund. We believe that we have made a significant step toward breaking down these barriers to full participation, but that there is still a long way to go, and that in future competitions, there will be even greater involvement of "nontraditional" players in competing for a center award.

1

Making It Happen: Setting the Federal Research Agenda

Anne P. Sweet
Judith I. Anderson
U.S. Department of Education

Setting a federal research agenda is not an easy task given the amount and diversity of educational research underway, work which represents varying perspectives and a broad range of research inquiry. Given limited resources, we had to make difficult choices about which research to support. No matter what amount of money is expended, researchers nearly always believe that more is needed. By and large, this may be true, and it makes our decisions about what to fund even more difficult, because there nearly always is more good research proposed than can be funded. From the very beginning of our planning, we had to confront a set of fairly basic questions: What research should we fund; whether we should fund a center for reading research; and, if we did, what kinds of research should be funded? The purpose of this book is threefold: to document the process we went through to answer these questions; to showcase the papers that helped guide the process; and to provide an introduction to the National Reading Research Center's work. We hope that the information in it will help those who are interested in entering future competitions.

Before we address the questions, we would like to note that completing the reading research center was a lengthy process—about 2 years from start to finish (see Fig. 1.1). Furthermore, we did not know the exact amount of money that would be available for the center until well into the process, an uncertainty which, if nothing else, ensured that we would not make an early commitment to a particular course of action. Given these uncertainties, what did we do?

Calendar Year		Activity
1990	March		Planning began
	...		
	August		Papers commissioned
	September		
	October	FY 1991 Begins	
	...		
1991	January		
	February		
	March		Public comments solicited
	April		AERA Roundtable
	May		IRA Panel
	June		
	July		Competition announced
	August		
	September		
	October	FY 1992 Begins	Proposals due to ED
	November		Peer review panel convened
	December		
1992	January		Negotiations with applicant
	February		Grant awarded
	March		R&D Center work began

FIG. 1.1.   Timeline for the National Reading Research Center Competition.

DECIDING WHAT RESEARCH TO FUND

We had fundamental decisions to make prior to beginning the process of shaping the mission for a new reading center. The former reading center, the Center for the Study of Reading (CSR), was not the only center to expire during this period of time. The Elementary School Subjects, Context of Secondary School Teaching, and two School Leadership Centers were scheduled to end at approximately the same time as the CSR. These centers also have their supporters and their own ongoing research. Our initial "reading" of the budget process was that we would have money for only one center. A decision to fund a reading center was a decision not to fund the other centers. It was also a decision against increasing funding for any of the other R&D centers that we support—24 in all. Any money spent on reading is money not spent on mathematics, or science, or teacher education, or any of the other areas in which educational research is being conducted today. The federal pot of money is limited and there is always great competition, not only between fields, but also among researchers within fields.

SHOULD WE FUND A CENTER
FOR READING RESEARCH?

Some members of the reading community may find it inconceivable that there would not be an NRRC. After all, there has been a federally funded reading research center for 15 years. Moreover, given the current concern over students' poor reading proficiency—as evidenced by results of the National Assessment of Educational Progress and a host of other studies— how could the Department even consider not having a reading center? Others, however, may see the need for reading research but not for an NRRC. They believe that the best way to support research and engender the maximum amount of original thinking is to support numerous independent researchers rather than place all funding under one roof. Still, others question the need for additional research in this area given that so much work has been done through the years. Isn't it time to take stock of what we already know and to put this knowledge to use in classrooms?

One approach to examining this issue was to take an abbreviated look at the CSR's accomplishments. Can a national reading center have a significant impact on the field? There is considerable evidence to show that it can. The former CSR, University of Illinois at Urbana-Champaign, has a plethora of accomplishments to its credit in terms of impact on U.S. schooling. And, it has produced key products aimed at broad audiences, a few of which are:

- *Becoming a Nation of Readers* (Anderson, Hiebert, Scott, & Wilkinson, 1985), commissioned through the National Academy of Education, continues to be widely read and cited. More than 300,000 copies of this book have been purchased by teachers and other educators and it has been used by many school districts and state departments of education as the basis of staff development for teachers, school administrators, and members of the business community.

- *10 Ways to Help Your Children Become Better Readers*, a pamphlet created at the CSR for use by parents, remains a popular publication, with more than 400,000 copies distributed. The pamphlet is available in both English and in Spanish.

- *Teachers and Independent Reading: Suggestions for the Classroom*, is a booklet produced specifically for elementary school teachers. The booklet contains ideas for ways teachers can incorporate more independent reading into their instruction, build classroom libraries, and work with others to promote independent reading, both in and out of school.

• *Beginning to Read: Thinking and Learning about Print* (Adams, 1990a, 1990b) is published both in book-length and summary form. The book, primarily aimed at researchers, reviews, evaluates, and synthesizes a wide range of often complex and technical research to show what is known about beginning reading and what is yet to be learned. The summary makes the findings of this research readily accessible to teachers, principals, and others who may be interested in beginning reading but who may not be specialists in the disciplines from which much of the research is drawn. The book and summary have prompted a national debate on the content of beginning reading instruction. To date, more than 35,000 copies of the summary have been sold.

• *A Guide to Selecting Basal Reading Programs*, is a series of nine booklets designed to help textbook adoption committees select the best reading program for the students who will be using them. Each booklet in the guide focuses on a key topic in reading instruction, including comprehension, workbooks, vocabulary instruction, selections in the basal reader, and tests. Each provides a brief review of pertinent research, offers guidelines for evaluation based on that research, and provides work sheets for organizing evaluation findings. Approximately 1,000 copies of the guide have been sold, and workshops featuring the guide and its use have been well received by teachers and reading specialists in several states.

• *Teaching Reading: Strategies from Successful Classrooms*, is a program of six videotapes featuring exemplary teachers conducting lessons in their own classrooms. In addition to the classroom footage, the tapes also contain discussions between the teachers and reading researchers about the strategies used. The tapes provide teacher educators with a wealth of material for classroom use with both preservice and experienced teachers. The program comes with viewers' and instructor's guides. Some 500 sets of tapes have been sold.

Clearly, a national reading center can effectively produce and disseminate research findings. Furthermore, such a center has the potential for fulfilling more functions than a series of small, individually funded research projects (see Fig. 1.2.). The former CSR did far more than conduct research:

• It served as a focal point for *informal exchange and collaboration*. This was accomplished through joint research efforts with researchers from other centers and universities.

• It exerted *intellectual influence* to effect changes that no single researcher could have brought about. Textbook adoption is one of the most powerful policy mechanisms that impact crucial decisions about how reading is taught. The CSR has had a significant impact on publishers' products through disseminating relevant research findings at sponsored conferences with the American Association of Publishers. Moreover, the

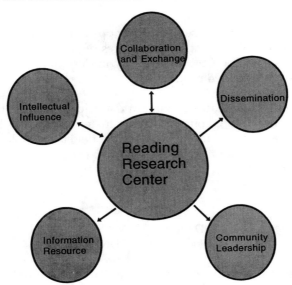

FIG. 1.2.   Functions of a research center.

CSR played an active role in the textbook adoption process in many state and local school districts. The center's *A Guide to Selecting Basal Reading Programs* has and is facilitating the textbook adoption process throughout the nation.

*   It worked aggressively to *disseminate* its findings by (a) conducting the Conference on Reading Research, which is a presession, primarily for practitioners, held before the annual IRA convention; (b) conducting summer institutes, *Becoming a School of Readers*, for practitioners throughout the nation; (c) presenting research findings at practitioner conferences such as the Association for Supervision and Curriculum Development (ASCD) and the National Association of Elementary School Principals (NAESP); and (d) leading inservice training sessions in states and school districts throughout the country—California, Colorado, Illinois, Massachusetts, Montana, Pennsylvania, Texas, and Virginia—to name a few locations.

*   It served not only as a *national resource center*, but also as an *international resource*. CSR's technical reports are still distributed on a regular basis throughout the United States, Great Britain, and Australia. Graduate students and researchers from these countries have and do participate in CSR programs. Marie Clay, who is credited with the development of the Reading Recovery Program, has spent time in residence at the CSR. The general public, as well as practitioners, still turn to CSR for the latest and best information about reading. This occurs partly because the CSR had a visibility that smaller groups of researchers and individuals cannot project.

*   It performed a *leadership role* for the practitioner and researcher

communities. The CSR staff served in key positions in all of the pertinent regional and national organizations—as presidents and chairpersons, and on editorial boards. The CSR led the way in designing theories and implementing research-based programs.

If we had not had a reading center in the field of reading, the ancillary functions described here could not have materialized. The likely result would have been a loss of momentum for the field as a whole and the loss of a major resource for the researcher and practitioner communities. Clearly, a national reading center can be larger than the sum of its research projects.

WHAT KIND OF READING RESEARCH SHOULD WE FUND?

Our challenge was to find a way to ensure that we captured a wide range of theoretical and practical perspectives and incorporated them into a well-balanced center mission statement. Because we couldn't talk to everyone individually, we had to find creative ways of tapping into the various constituencies, still ensuring that those individuals who are not represented by traditional interest groups could be heard.

First, we planned a number of activities to set the stage. In preparation for this competition, we sought to raise the levels of awareness on the part of reading and literacy researchers and practitioners by conducting planning activities that included the following:

• In August 1990, we commissioned papers, which comprise the major portion of this book, from six experts in the literacy field. These six, who include both researchers and practitioners, are: Richard C. Anderson, a professor and director of the Center for the Study of Reading at the University of Illinois at Urbana-Champaign; Isabel L. Beck, a senior scientist at the Learning Research and Development Center (LRDC), University of Pittsburgh; Joy N. Monahan, a reading consultant for the Orange County Public Schools in Orlando, Florida; Peter B. Mosenthal, professor and chair of the Reading Language Arts Center at Syracuse University; Sara I. Scroggins, an independent literacy consultant in St. Louis, Missouri; and Elizabeth Sulzby, a professor at the School of Education at the University of Michigan. Prospective authors were selected because of their (a) prominence in the field; (b) proven scholarship in area of expertise; and (c) ability to write for a wide variety of audiences. We also chose individuals whose collective range in expertise spans preschool through secondary school and beyond.

• In the spring of 1991, we solicited comments from the public at large on needed research by placing advertisements in the *Chronicle of Higher*

Education, Education Week, Reading Today, U.S. Department of Education's Office of Educational Research and Improvement (OERI) Bulletin, and the *Federal Register*. The comments we received, along with the other information we collected, was used to develop a mission statement for the NRRC.

• We held a roundtable discussion at the annual meeting of the American Educational Research Association (AERA) in April 1991 where we solicited members' views on projecting a reading research agenda into the year 2000. It was a highly charged, standing room only session, where participants advanced strong views on lines of inquiry for future research on reading.

• We conducted a cosponsored session with the International Reading Association (IRA) at their annual convention in May 1991, where the six authors discussed their views on the direction that federally sponsored research on reading should take. This session drew a "full house" of enthusiasts whose only regret was that the time allotted to this session was much too brief.

The professional education public—teachers, school and school district supervisors and administrators, researchers—responded with a great deal of enthusiasm. Moreover, the consistency of response was remarkable. In brief, the overwhelming majority of persons who participated in these activities was in favor of OERI's continued support for reading research.

Common themes for topics of study were evident. Major themes included reading and learning from content text and textbooks in other school subjects; instructional strategies for at-risk students (e.g., culturally and linguistically diverse); evaluation of instructional approaches (e.g., whole language); alternative assessments (e.g., portfolios); teacher education and instructional interventions (e.g., Reading Recovery); and studies that investigate rigorously and simultaneously the cultural, social (including motivational), and cognitive aspects of reading acquisition and the contexts within which reading takes place.

Was this a perfect strategy? No. We would like in the future to try to get a wider range of respondents, particularly representative of parents and teachers. We would like to have advertised in magazines that are apt to be read by these groups—*Redbook, Family Circle, Parents Magazine, Teacher Magazine*. We did explore placing an ad in *Teacher Magazine*; the cost was prohibitive. We also would like to have held widely advertised regional forums, but, again, we did not have the resources. Some of these "holes" in strategy were filled by our ongoing contacts with the field. In addition, we review much of the correspondence that is sent to the President, the Secretary of Education, and members of Congress that is related to education. Our job as federal employees is to draft replies to such correspondence as directed, and in doing so, learn about the concerns of the public and of special interest groups.

Based on all of the information that we accrued, as well as our knowledge of the field, we developed the mission statement for the NRRC grants announcement. The grants announcement became available on July 17, 1991, with a closing date of October 18, 1991.

THE NATIONAL READING RESEARCH
CENTER MISSION STATEMENT

Before we talk a little bit about the mission for the NRRC that was set forth in the grants announcement, we would be remiss if we didn't comment on the current state of literacy affairs in our nation. As we enter the 21st century, our current generation must become literate enough to meet the demands of the future—and this can't happen soon enough. The admonition set forth by the National Academy of Education's Commission on Reading in its landmark report, *Becoming a Nation of Readers*, rings true as urgently today as it did when these words were first written in 1985. It says, and we quote: "The world is moving into a technological-information age in which full participation in education, science, business, industry, and the professions requires increasing levels of literacy. What was a satisfactory level of literacy in 1950 probably will be marginal by the year 2000" (p. 3).

It is clear that we must accelerate the pace toward reaching substantially higher levels of reading proficiency dramatically if we are to achieve the national education goals within the timelines specified.

All of those involved with improving education count on education research to guide them in their judgments. Education research can contribute to the improvement of teaching and learning in schools, and research on reading has provided the basis for some of the most significant contributions. These contributions interface with the cognitive revolution that has unfolded during the previous two decades to influence profoundly instruction and schooling.

An explosion of knowledge has accrued about how people learn, remember, and reason. We have learned much about the knowledge and abilities that distinguish experts from novices. We have learned much about how people learn in school as compared to the real world. We have learned much about self-regulation and how it is a key aspect of skilled reading. There remains much more to be learned about these and related understandings, and the unique role each one plays in students' acquisition of reading proficiency.

SCOPE OF NRRC ACTIVITIES

Now we turn to the scope of the NRRC activities that we posed in the grants announcement. We envisioned that the NRRC would engage in research aimed at improving the reading proficiency of all students, and thereby, improving the nation's level of literacy. The NRRC would strive to develop a broad, comprehensive model of reading acquisition that integrates the various cognitive, social, motivational, cultural, and instructional elements that play a role in learning to read and the reading process. Within this framework, the NRRC's primary objective would be to understand more fully how students learn to read, the strategies they use as they become better readers, their use of acquired reading skills in learning content knowledge, and the myriad of factors that influence the acquisition and development of reading proficiency, including the context in which reading takes place. A second objective was to better understand the reading process—particularly as it pertains to students at risk for reading failure—the relevance of reading to learning content subjects, and the relationship between reading and writing, and other literacy skills. A third objective was to understand more fully the phenomenon of current instructional trends and interventions, including issues related to the education of teachers, the implementation of new teaching models and instructional strategies, and the evaluation of instruction and student progress.

The National Reading Research Center would engage in (a) systematic, longer term research aimed at broadening our understanding of the many aspects of reading and expanding the theories on which future research may be based; and (b) shorter term research aimed at improving the teaching and learning of reading in U.S. schools. The student populations to be studied included students from diverse cultural and linguistic backgrounds at all grade levels, prekindergarten through high school.

The scope of NRRC activities would embrace at least three major program areas—learning, instruction, and assessment. It was structured this way because of the unique role that each of these elements can play in planning a comprehensive reading research agenda.

Learning

First, there is learning. We know that the ability to read is key to enabling students to succeed in and out of school. An important prerequisite for improving the literacy level of all learners is an understanding of how students become proficient readers. We need to understand more about how students learn to acquire new knowledge in other school subjects through reading content texts. An important prerequisite for raising the reading proficiency level of all students is to understand how best to engage them in learning to read and reading to learn.

Areas of inquiry critical to improving students' ability to read include:

- How students learn school subjects (e.g., history and science) from textbooks.
- Early literacy learning and the relative influence of home, school, and community.

Instruction

Second, there is instruction. We know that effective reading instruction involves far more than teaching decoding. Students should be taught how to interact with text, using all available sources of information to create meaning from what they read. Within the reading context, they should be taught to set reading goals based on purposes for reading, draw upon their background knowledge, make inferences, and analyze and evaluate information on the printed page. They should be taught to recognize the structure of text as an aid to understanding what they read. Moreover, they should be taught to monitor their understanding of what they read and employ "fix-up" strategies when their comprehension fails.

Areas of inquiry critical to promoting effective teaching of reading include:

- The ways in which new instructional approaches (e.g., whole language, phonemic awareness training) affect beginning readers, particularly at-risk learners.
- Instructional strategies that facilitate learning from text and textbooks in content area school subjects.
- Models that connect effective teaching practices and the education of teachers, both preservice and inservice.

Assessment

The last area is assessment. We know that the assessment of students' ability to read will continue to play a dominant role in society's need to gauge the effectiveness of reading instruction in U.S. schools, students' aptitude for academic learning up through postsecondary education, and students' readiness to enter the work force.

Today, we are moving away from measuring students' reading achievement by using multiple-choice items based on short passages. We are beginning to ask students to perform more authentic activities. Students are being asked to read longer passages and write about what they have read. They are assessed with a wider variety of text types. They are asked questions that require them to think about the meaning of the text, not just answer factual questions.

Given the variety of decisions that are made about students, schools, and schooling, based on reading test scores, it is critical that assessments of reading proficiency reflect our current understanding about what constitutes the act of reading. More and better reading assessments for multiple purposes are on the horizon.

Areas of inquiry critical to promoting the development of authentic reading proficiency measures include:

- The effectiveness of current and new measures of reading proficiency.

- Measures of reading proficiency that help teachers improve instruction.
- Reading assessments that provide parents and policymakers with accurate information about students' progress.

EXPECTATIONS FOR THE NRRC

The OERI had definitive expectations for the plan of operations in the new NRRC. The NRRC was expected to embrace the belief that theory must be grounded in practice. Moreover, researchers and practitioners could assume alternating roles—that is, researchers and practitioners would be equally teacher and learner, leader and follower. We believed that collaborations among teacher–researcher colleagues could increase the likelihood that the fruits of the NRRC's research will be assimilated readily into everyday practice in classrooms.

The NRRC was also expected to exhibit a commitment to nurturing a program of research that is multidimensional and interdisciplinary. The NRRC would integrate divergent views and study the development of reading proficiency from multiple perspectives—cognitive, linguistic, sociocultural, and contextual.

SELECTING THE WINNER

Some readers may believe that the federal government independently selects the winners for the NRRC competitions. We do not. We use a peer review for all of our NRRC grant competitions. Who is a peer? What is a peer review process?

Peer review is a process whereby external—non-Department of Education—experts serve on a panel to read, review, and evaluate the proposals that are submitted in an R&D center grant competition. Selecting the panel members is never easy. There are always problems finding good people who are knowledgeable about the research area but who are not involved in the competition. Most applications for R&D center grants are from consortia of research institutions. Commonly, applicants have a wide array of advisors, including researchers, practitioners, and policymakers. All of the individuals named in the proposals are ineligible to serve on the panel because of a conflict of interest caused by their affiliation with the applicants. Now, realize that we select the peer review panel *before* we receive the applications. We don't know who will be ineligible until we start calling potential reviewers.

Peer review panels are usually composed of seven members—typically four researchers, two practitioners, and one policymaker. Finding seven knowledgeable people who represent these categories and who are not involved with any of the applicants is a tall order. For the NRRC competition, we called more than 100 potential reviewers. It was not an easy process, but we managed to assemble a first-rate panel. And, by the end of the process, we also had a very good idea of who the applicants were going to be, and who all of their consultants and collaborators were.

We told each panelist approximately when we would send them the proposals, and how long they would have to read and rate them prior to assembling in Washington, DC in November 1991, for the panel meeting. We sent them background material, including the grant announcement, which contained the evaluation criteria, the mission statement for the NRRC, and instructions to applicants. We informed each of them that they would be evaluating the proposals based on rating criteria that were published in the grant announcement. These evaluation criteria are established by regulation. They were used for all of the previous 24 center competitions, not just for the NRRC competition. If we had wanted to change them, we would have had to write new regulations and go through the entire Notice of Proposed Rule Making process—which can be a very lengthy process. It is not unusual for this process to take a year or more.

Two weeks before the panel was scheduled to meet, we sent panelists the six eligible proposals for review. These proposals were fairly lengthy. We imposed a 200-page limit on the proposal narrative. Be mindful that with six proposals, that is 1,200 pages of reading for reviewers who got paid very little for the entire review, who have full-time jobs, and who had only 2 weeks to complete their initial reviews. They surely participated out of love, not money. We instructed the reviewers to do initial ratings—including not only the scores but also the written commentary to support the assigned scores—prior to their arrival in Washington. They were to work independently, although they knew who the other reviewers were.

In November 1992, the peer review meeting unfolded in the following way. After introductory remarks by the director of the Office of Research, the OERI panel liaison rendered an overview of the review process and instructions to panelists for completing their evaluations. The meeting was then turned over to the panel chairperson, who established the procedures for panel deliberations. We cannot tell you who the reviewers were or who the applicants were (except for the winner) because we protect their right to privacy. In brief:

- Reviewers were instructed to keep the panel's deliberations confidential.
- Preliminary scores were collected initially, and at periodic intervals throughout the panel meeting.
- Each application was reviewed systematically, in a like manner:
  - The lead reviewer assigned to the application presented an overview of the proposal.
  - Then, the panel discussed the applicant's strengths and

weaknesses, by criterion.
- Final scores were collected and tabulated.
- Issues for negotiations were formulated for the two applications that received the highest scores.

The panel's job was extremely difficult because competition for the NRRC award was very keen—keener than it had been since the inception of a federally funded reading research center some 15 years ago. It is clear that a great deal of enthusiasm had been sparked in the reading education and research communities.

Next, the panel liaison summarized the panel's findings, which included their recommendation to the Assistant Secretary regarding which proposal to fund for an NRRC. The Assistant Secretary of OERI makes the final award recommendation to the U.S. Department of Education's Grants and Contracts Service (GCS). Although the Assistant Secretary is at liberty to choose an awardee different from the peer review panel's recommendation, this almost never happens. He or she takes the review panel's recommendation very seriously—relying heavily on the panel's advise before making an informed choice.

After a careful review of the panelists' recommendations, the OERI Assistant Secretary concurred with their findings. Her decision was sent to GCS for action. Before the award could be made, we needed to negotiate several issues with the potential awardee. Seldom do we receive a grant application that is funded "as is." The reviewers nearly always identify problematic areas that need to be resolved before the award is made. We resolve these issues through negotiations: a series of give-and-take written exchanges between the granter and the likely grantee. Questions are posed to the potential awardee about the activities contained in the proposal. Sometimes these questions, which originate from the peer review panel and OERI, are posed to gain additional information about particular aspects of what has been proposed. At other times, these questions are targeted at correcting minor flaws in the details of what the applicant has proposed.

Because the NRRC award was set up as a cooperative agreement, the negotiations were more extensive than if the award were a "straight" grant. What is a *cooperative agreement?* It's a special kind of grant that provides for a partnership between the grantor (Department of Education, OERI) and the grantee (the winning applicant). This type of grant opens the door for the grantor and the grantee to work collaboratively on the full range of R&D center activities. Because of this collaboration, negotiations are often fairly extensive.

Once the Office of Research, OERI, is satisfied that all of the issues for negotiation have been resolved satisfactorily, GCS is given the signal to proceed on reaching closure. Grants and Contracts has a special role to play in all of this—GCS scrutinizes the intended awardee's budget and makes sure that everything is in order. Next, the director of the Grants Division,

GCS, signs an official document, in this case the cooperative agreement document, which renders the award legal and valid. The last step before the awardee receives official notification via receipt of this document is for the Department to notify Congress. Congressional notification precedes awardee notification by five days. In this way, Congress has an opportunity to announce the R&D center award and the identity of the recipient. At this point, the award becomes public information and the Department of Education usually sends out a national press release. Finally, the awardee is free to tell the world about its good fortune.

On March 1, 1992, the NRRC began work. The NRRC award went to the University of Georgia (UGA)–University of Maryland at College Park (UMCP) consortium. The co-directors are Donna Alvermann (UGA) and John T. Guthrie (UMCP).

Dr. Alvermann is a professor of reading education and the director of the Cognitive Studies Group in the Institute for Behavioral Research at the University of Georgia. Dr. Guthrie is a professor of human development and the director of the Center for Educational Research and Development at the University of Maryland at College Park.

The following chapters include the commissioned papers that provided the background for the NRRC mission statement contained in the grant application package prepared by the Department of Education for the competition. The final chapter focuses on the winner's reading research agenda.

Richard C. Anderson discusses the future of reading research from the perspective of the director of the incumbent CSR. Dr. Anderson reviews the state of the art in reading research, discusses differing visions of education reform, and proposes criteria for selecting research projects before suggesting directions for research and development. His suggestions include the nature of reading, learning to read and write, the acquisition of knowledge, critical reading and thinking (metacognition), and the education of reading teachers.

Elizabeth Sulzby focuses primarily on young children through the elementary school years, but with a life-span developmental perspective. She stresses the need to keep the doors open to all kinds of reading and writing experiences for all children to the greatest extent possible. Dr. Sulzby sees a need to keep theoretical perspectives, research designs, and instructional implementations with both a proximal and distal focus: on the child in the immediate context and on the child as he or she may be in the far future as a result of our theory, research, and instruction.

Isabel Beck discusses two theoretical orientations (cognitive and social) that have influenced both theory and practice and follows with a discussion of research on comprehension in which the two theoretical orientations emerge. She concludes the discussion with perspectives on setting a research agenda before moving on to a review of recent developments in research on the nature of texts and concluding observations about future

research. In her third section, Dr. Beck focuses on topics related to instruction in beginning reading and on key concerns now confronting this issue.
She ends with her recommendations for a reading research agenda.

Joy Monahan, as a practitioner, has a pragmatic approach. She is concerned that research focus on how to teach complex concepts to all students—at risk, minorities, disadvantaged, culturally diverse, and gifted.
She asserts that professional growth and development of teachers occur as
they tackle those tasks and learn to use technology effectively to enhance
student learning. She is also a strong proponent of ethnographic research
and of teachers as researchers. Mrs. Monahan points out that there are many
sound reading research findings available now, which could help practitioners, and that making these findings readily available should be a
primary objective.

Sara Scroggins also provides a practitioner's perspective—a practitioner
who has been a classroom teacher, reading specialist, and administrator for
the past 37 years in a large, urban school district. Her principal concern is
for inner-city children, who are disproportionately represented in special
education classes, school dropout statistics, low-level academic tracking
programs, remedial reading classes, and inadequately financed schools.
Her experiences demonstrate to her that inner-city children can succeed in
reading if given the same educational opportunities on a daily basis that
children who are not at risk are offered. Mrs. Scroggins concurs that there
is an abundance of potentially helpful research findings on teaching methods, strategies, materials, effective schools, effective teachers, ethnic
groups, and appropriate curriculum. She asserts that now is the time to
implement the research recommendations and evaluate the results.

Peter Mosenthal describes how agendas in reading research tend to be
set before identifying three perspectives that frame goal and problem
identification in the setting of reading research agendas. He argues that
reading researchers, in setting their agendas, tended to ignore the "ends"
aspect of agenda setting and focused largely on the means. Moreover, they
tended to define problems and goals locally, largely motivated by theoretical
concerns rather than by actual situations. He discusses three agenda-setting
perspectives: an administrative-efficiency perspective; a client-satisfaction
perspective; and an emancipationist perspective. Each has a significantly
different set of goals and problems, which, in turn, suggest very different
ends of what should be included on a reading research agenda.

In the last chapter, the co-directors of the recently awarded National
Reading Research Center, Donna Alvermann and John Guthrie, address the
degree to which the NRRC is responsive to the perspectives of fellow
authors in this volume. They also discuss the NRRC's research programs
and related activities, which focus on:

- *Instruction* in reading that fosters learning and thinking in literature,
  science, and history.

- *Learning* to read in homes, schools, and communities.
- *Assessment* that supports the improvement of teaching and learning.
- *Development* of teacher–researcher communities that promote professionalism in reading.

The NRRC research in these areas is guided by an engagement perspective, which seeks to develop motivated readers who learn from and respond to texts in diverse settings for a variety of purposes. Doctor Alvermann and Dr. Guthrie expound on this notion.

REFERENCES

A Guide to Selecting Basal Reading Programs. (Guide prepared through U.S. Department of Education, OERI, cooperative agreement No. G0087-C1001, Reading Research & Education Center). Urbana-Champaign, IL: Center for the Study of Reading.

Application for a Grant Under the Educational Research and Development Centers Program (Office of Research, OERI, CFDA No. 84.117A). Washington, DC: U.S. Department of Education.

Adams, M. J. (1990a). *Beginning to read: Thinking and learning about print.* Cambridge, MA: MIT Press.

Adams, M. J. (1990b). *Beginning to read: Thinking and learning about print, A summary.* (Summary prepared by S. A. Stahl, J. Osborn, & F. Lehr.) Urbana-Champaign, IL: Center for the Study of Reading.

Anderson, R. C., Heibert, E. H., Scott, J. A., & Wilkinson, I. A. G. (1985). *Becoming a nation of readers: The report of the commission on reading.* Washington, DC: National Institute of Education.

Teachers and Independent Reading: Suggestions for the Classroom. (Booklet prepared through U.S. Department of Education, OERI, cooperative agreement No. G0087-C1001, Reading Research & Education Center) Urbana-Champaign, IL: Center for the Study of Reading.

Teaching Reading: Strategies from Successful Classrooms. (Videotape series prepared through U.S. Department of Education, OERI, cooperative agreement No. G0087-C1001, Reading Research & Education Center, with funds from the Exxon Education Foundation et al.) Urbana-Champaign, IL: Center for the Study of Reading.

10 Ways to Help Your Children Become Better Readers. (Brochure prepared through U.S. Department of Education, OERI, cooperative agreement No. G0087-C1001, Reading Research & Education Center). Urbana-Champaign, IL: Center for the Study of Reading.

2

The Future of Reading Research

Richard C. Anderson
University of Illinois at Urbana-Champaign

Reading is not a neutral topic. Any program of research and development in reading must be conceived in full knowledge that reading has extraordinary consequences for individual people and for the nation. And, it must be conceived with the understanding that reading is a public concern. Citizens know reading is important. They care passionately that their children learn to read. Many have strongly held beliefs about how reading should be taught.

Ordinary citizens and scholars alike agree that reading is the essential prerequisite for school achievement, as well as eventual personal and economic success. The child who succeeds in learning to read finds other school subjects accessible, but the child who cannot read well is certain to encounter difficulty.

Every first grader knows that you go to school to learn to read. Children who accomplish this rite of passage feel good about themselves. Children who fail experience low self-esteem and frequently become unpopular among their classmates. There is a depressing stability to test scores and other educational indicators after the first grade: The first grader who cannot independently read stories from the first reader by the end of the year is already at grave risk for school failure.

Children from any walk of life may face difficulty in learning to read. However, the incidence of slow progress and outright failure is highest among poor children, children from homes low in literacy, ethnic minority children, and children who have limited proficiency in English. Children who become accomplished readers despite these life circumstances have a springboard for breaking the cycle of ignorance and poverty. But those who make unsatisfactory progress in reading become even more vulnerable to failing in school, dropping out, and the accompanying social risks. The highest priority for reading research and development should be to discover and put into practice the means for reaching children who are failing to learn to read.

Many children who have learned to read, at least in a rudimentary way, are unable to use what they have learned to unlock the secrets of science, history, and other subjects. Part of the problem is school textbooks. Far too many textbooks are disgracefully written, superficial baskets of facts. A root cause of the problem is that too many classrooms are not places that "rouse children's minds to life" (Tharp & Gallimore, 1988). Consequently, students may not appreciate what it means to have a conceptual understanding of an area of knowledge. They may not know how to go about acquiring knowledge. A high priority for reading research and development should be to discover how to help all children acquire knowledge from the written word.

STATE OF THE ART IN READING RESEARCH

Research made considerable progress over the last 15 years in illuminating the process of reading. There are several reasons for this, not the least of which is a greater federal investment in reading research. But, perhaps the major reason for rapid progress is the paradigm shift in psychology and allied disciplines. In the field of reading, the fruits of the "cognitive revolution" are now everywhere to be seen. It should be a point of honor among people in this field that reading researchers were among the leaders in developing the new cognitive view.

The very conception of reading, learning to read, and the teaching of reading are changing, thanks in considerable measure to research that flies the banner of cognitive science. It is now widely understood that readers "construct" the meanings of texts. That is to say, it is generally accepted that the building blocks for the meaning of a text include, not only the words on its pages, but the reader's purposes and point of view, analysis of the context and author's intentions, and already possessed knowledge and belief about the topic. Skilled readers swiftly and effortlessly integrate information from various sources as they build a representation of a text.

Extending the idea of constructivism, previously separate strands of research and theory recently have been amalgamated under the banner of social constructivism. Espousing this idea are not only psychologists and computer scientists, but also anthropologists, linguists, political scientists, and literary theorists. The central idea is that the individual is the creature of culture and, thus, that learning and development must be construed as socially situated. Following the Russian psychologist, Vygotsky, the premise is that children acquire the ways of thinking of those around them by internalizing speech patterns. This premise motivates the close analysis of the talk between parent and child and teacher and child.

Other powerful ideas with origins in recent scholarship that are influencing reading education include the notions of phonemic awareness, automaticity, schema, and metacognition. Although these ideas have had wide currency in reading education, they are still working their way into the field's consciousness. Likewise, whereas there has already been some successful use of the ideas in instructional materials and teaching methods, the potential has hardly begun to be realized.

Inevitably, there has been some misinterpretation and overextension of ideas from recent research, in part because the ideas themselves are still being refined. The idea of automaticity, for instance, has been unpacked into subconcepts. The idea of a schema has proved to be too brittle to explain how people cope with novel situations, and is now taking a back seat to the notion of mental models that are cut and fit in particular circumstances of use. Science marches on and concepts are modified or replaced.

For illustration, one achievement of the past 15 years was the clear articulation of the structure of simple stories and how implicit knowledge of this structure assists comprehension, learning, and remembering. Analysis of stories using the tools of cognitive science did not begin until the mid-1970s. Yet the bibliography in a recent review of story research lists over 100 books and articles with publication dates after 1975.

The structure of stories was represented in so-called story grammars that decompose stories into major plot elements. Research showed that the concept of a story grammar has psychological reality. For example, when stories are rewritten so that elements are out of order, people shuffle the elements back into the right order when asked to recall the stories. Studies showed that children taught a story grammar are better able to comprehend stories, and when composing stories of their own are more likely to make them complete. Contradicting the often-expressed view that in education implementing research takes interminable lengths of time, research on stories had an almost immediate impact. Probably a large proportion of the primary school teachers in the country is familiar with research on story structure and uses it in teaching.

A second round of story research revealed complexities overlooked in the initial rush of enthusiasm. By the standards of what counts as a grammar of sentences, theories of story structure are not really grammars. The theories cannot account for the structure of stories of any complexity, for instance, those involving multiple episodes or many characters. The early theories did not deal with the point, or moral, of stories. The early theories of stories did not take account of the fact that stories are usually structured so as to evoke feelings of curiosity, surprise, or suspense. Again, science moves on; in an active field of inquiry, research is usually self-correcting.

The fear is sometimes voiced that premature application of research will have a mischievous effect on educational practice. The practical application of early story research had benefits, despite its limitations. There is no evidence that overly simple models blinded teachers and children to the richness and complexity of literature or prevented them from pursuing deeper meanings. Rather, the evidence is that ideas from story research helped teachers help children to better understand stories.

DIFFERING VISIONS OF EDUCATIONAL REFORM

Most teachers, principals, and college faculty concerned with reading can be described as eclectic. They pragmatically consider ideas and approaches to teaching from various sources. Whereas this may seem an unexceptionable and professional attitude, it is regarded with suspicion by the ideologically committed. By their lights, typical reading educators are the ones who need to be "reformed."

One group of reformers believes that the root cause of reading failure is lack of phonics. This group contends that children will get off to a better start as readers if they first receive systematic and intensive phonics instruction. In fact, reviews of research over the years consistently concluded that, on the average, children who receive phonics instruction do make somewhat better progress in reading.

Whether more phonics is a cure for what ails us is another matter, however. Indeed, whether direct instruction in letter sound relationships will ultimately prove to be the best way to get children started in reading must be regarded as an open question. Seldom acknowledged by "phonics firsters" is the fact that most children in most classrooms in the United States do receive a lot of phonics instruction. An unacceptably large number of children who receive direct phonics instruction do not learn to read well.

As an issue, phonics is at a low ebb among teachers and other reading educators. One reason for the low ebb is that professionals regard the emphasis on a single issue as simplistic; they have seen lots of children who mastered the sounds of letters but who cannot figure out unfamiliar words. Another reason is the xenophobia of some phonics advocates and the rancor with which they press their case. A third reason is the rise of a very different reform movement whose rallying cry is "whole language."

Whole language is a crusade at high tide. Defining whole language is difficult, because advocates insist that it is a philosophy, not a method. Of course, one of the central ideas is that learning to read should be addressed holistically, specifically that reading should not be broken down into component skills that are taught one at a time. This means whole language advocates are against phonics instruction, at least as it is traditionally done. Other features of the philosophy include the belief that learning to read should be natural, like learning to talk, and that children should learn to read from authentic texts, which are to be distinguished from made-for-school texts. Since the rise of whole language, we are to say "emergent literacy" instead of "beginning reading." Whole language teachers cultivate literacy rich environments; they seldom, if ever, engage in direct instruction. Whole language stands for empowering the disenfranchised. Administrators and other authority figures, basal reading programs, and the "system" are regarded as usurping prerogatives that rightfully belong to teachers, and ultimately to the young.

Spokespersons for whole language insist that taking a position on an issue in literacy is always a political act. Regrettably, as if to prove the point, some of the most visible advocates of whole language have proved no less intemperate and rancorous than the phonics firsters. Yet, the features of whole language are not bound together by logical necessity. Many of the features are independently endorsed by reading educators who do not consider themselves to be part of the whole language movement. Among eclectics, at least, a literacy rich environment and direct instruction go together without contradiction. Among those known for their advocacy of systematic phonics, instruction in letter sound correspondences is not seen as inconsistent with a commitment to authentic literature.

If winning the allegiance of teachers is the criterion, whole language is a success. The philosophy is espoused by increasing numbers of teachers from every region of the country; in many quarters, it is simply taken for granted that whole language is the standard for what is good practice in reading and language arts. There is no question that, in many respects, the influence of whole language has been positive. For instance, the movement is an effective force against some of the worst features of conventional reading instruction, such as overreliance on workbooks and skill sheets. The whole language movement deserves part of the credit for the surge in the amount of writing children do in elementary school classrooms around the country. By other criteria, the evaluation of whole language is less certain. Most worrisome, there is research that suggests a high incidence of failures to learn to read in whole language classrooms among children who enter first grade with the least understanding of literacy.

Actually, for several reasons, research on whole language is inconclusive. If it is a philosophy, not a method, then empirical research seems pointless, or so some believe. Whole language spokespersons are suspicious of quantitative and experimental methods. They reject tests, most especially standardized tests, because, they say, tests fragment literacy and because taking a test is not an authentic literacy experience. Moreover, in the eyes of some, eschewing tests is a political imperative because tests are tools of the establishment. In the place of quantitative comparisons, case studies are offered that paint a pleasing picture of the whole language classroom. To the complaint that case studies are inconclusive and susceptible to subjective interpretation, the reply is that whole language has to be judged on its own terms.

The dispute over what to weigh as evidence in decisions about phonics, whole language, and other issues in reading is just one installment in a continuing debate about goals and methods in educational research. The methods of educational research have been the methods of social science, which, in turn, have been heavily influenced by the philosophy and methods of the natural sciences. This can be called the tradition of *scientific research.*

Now an alternative approach, termed by one authority *interpretative scholarship*, is challenging the hegemony of scientific research in education. The distinctive feature of interpretative scholarship is that it aims to describe the meanings of events from the point of view of the participants. This first person point of view is to be distinguished from the third person point of view taken in scientific research, as signified, for instance, by the use of the term *subject* to refer to a participant in a scientific study. Interpretive scholarship involves qualitative methods, which are drawn from several disciplines, notably anthropology.

What is the proper form and what are the proper methods for educational research? Polemicists on both sides of this issue argue there is only one way. I believe there is a good case for both approaches. To those who say scientific research is the only way, my reply is that interpretative scholarship can enrich understanding and allow issues to be addressed that are difficult to examine in scientific research. To those who say interpretive scholarship is the only way, my rejoinder is that this dismisses a tradition of scholarship with several centuries of success behind it, including palpable achievements within education.

Debates about philosophy of science and research methods aside, the field desperately needs research to decide among alternative proposals for reading and writing instruction. To be deflected from doing the research, or to fail to insist that research be considered in decisions about curriculum and methods in reading and writing, on the grounds that the research will not persuade ideologues, is tantamount to allowing ideology to prevail over rational and empirical analysis.

CRITERIA FOR SELECTING RESEARCH PROJECTS

It would seem natural to expect children who are failing to learn to read to continue to make slow progress. However, in Reading Recovery, the successful program for poor-performing first graders, teachers are taught to expect the opposite. A key to the accelerated progress achieved in Reading Recovery is the use of "powerful examples." Powerful examples allow a child to leap ahead by illuminating regions at the frontiers of the child's understanding. For example, to become a good reader, the child must start seeing the clusters of letters in words rather than looking at them letter by letter. Suppose a child reading a story pauses at *should*, having easily read *could* a few pages earlier. Then the following might serve as a powerful example for this child: Teacher prints *could* on the chalk board and says, "You know *could* (pointing to *could*), don't you? If this is could, what is this (pointing to *should* in the child's book)?" In general, for an example to be powerful, it must arise during a teachable moment, connect with the child's current developmental level, and be handled deftly. The child may not say, "Eureka," but if the episode is successful he or she will have made a discovery about letter clusters. A powerful example at a propitious moment can do more to spur growth in reading than hours of ill-timed, generic drill and practice.

Similarly, greater progress in research and development comes from powerful science than grinding, normal science. Powerful science is more likely when scientists and those who sponsor science observe the following criteria:

- *The priority criterion:* Attack the most important problems.
- *The knowledge criterion:* Attack problems whose solution will lead to the greatest advance in knowledge.
- *The feasibility criterion:* Attack problems the field can solve.
- *The implementation criterion:* Attack problems whose solutions can be implemented readily.

What is implied by the priority criterion and the knowledge criterion is, perhaps, self-evident, although thoughtful application of these criteria requires acute judgment. Maybe this is the reason the criteria are so imperfectly honored.

Honoring the feasibility criterion means paying attention to the number and quality of trained personnel in a specialty and the promise of the ideas and methods they are able to bring to bear. In my judgment, educational research often flounders on the shoal of the feasibility criterion. The relevant disciplines lack the conceptual or methodological tools to seriously address the problem, or there are not enough people who possess the tools who are interested in working on the problem.

Honoring the implementation criterion might mean, for instance, making a disproportionate investment in research on textbooks, even though textbooks are a much less important influence on children's learning than the quality of teaching they receive. Only 100 or so publishing company executives need to understand and accept a finding in order for it to get into widespread practice. Reaching the minds and hearts of 1 million school teachers is a far greater task.

SOME DIRECTIONS FOR RESEARCH
AND DEVELOPMENT

This section describes programs of research and development in reading that, in my judgment, are highly likely to advance knowledge and educational practice. The list that follows is not exhaustive; there are other worthy projects that could be added. Described are programs of research, instead of individual studies, because complicated problems are seldom solved in single studies; ordinarily substantial progress requires a cumulative series of studies. The principle for ordering the programs in the following list is that the earlier programs are in one sense or another foundational for the later ones.

The Nature of Reading

Reading is a dynamic activity that unfolds in time, with different types of processes occurring at different moments. What we comprehend after having read a passage is the result of these moment-by-moment activities. To understand reading, in the ultimate sense, is to understand the nature of these activities: what they are, when they occur, how they are controlled, what visual and stored information are involved in them, how they change with instruction and experience. To understand reading development, in this sense, is to understand the difference in these processes between the child and the adult.

Considerable progress has been made during the past 15 years in understanding the moment-by-moment dynamics of reading. The field is now at the point where formal models of a number of aspects of the process are being proposed and tested. But answers to a number of important questions are still incomplete: What are the perceptual processes that take place during eye fixations in reading? What is entailed in word identification? What are the processes required for the representation of the meaning of propositions? Which of many possible inferences will be made during reading? How do readers construct summaries of texts? How do readers build representations of the situations described in texts? Answering these questions must be a high priority for reading research.

More is known from research about skilled adult reading than about the reading of young children. For example, when compared to adults, there are puzzling aspects to children's perceptual activities during reading. Adults typically fix the eyes on a word just once during reading. Children, however, tend to direct the eyes to the same word for several fixations; yet if the word is changed between fixations (by means of a computer) they are frequently unaware that this has happened. Children display many very short eye movements, often keeping the eyes on the same letter. The suspicion is that there is a developing coordination between visual attention and higher level language processes. Children's perceptual processes during reading are in need of further study. In general, there is a need for developmental studies of dynamic processes during reading.

Research-based knowledge constrains, or should constrain, discussions of instructional materials and teaching techniques. For example, some approaches to teaching reading have been justified on the basis that "reading is a psycholinguistic guessing game" that involves sampling letters and words to confirm hypotheses. Research clearly demonstrates that reading is no such thing; skilled readers use virtually all of the information in the letters and words on a page. Other approaches to teaching reading appeal to the premise that identifying words entails recoding them into speech. This premise, too, is false; research informs us that skilled readers do not ordinarily, necessarily, translate words into speech before accessing their meanings.

I feel it is necessary to sound an alarm about the increasing gulf between scientific research and discussions of how reading and writing are acquired and how they should be taught. There are several reasons for this gulf. One reason is the rise of interpretative scholarship mentioned earlier. This form of scholarship has a large following in the literacy field. Whatever its true merit, it has a seductive appeal for the scientifically uneducated who can, if they embrace this approach, excuse themselves from the technical rigors of science. A second reason is that, especially since the dawn of neural network theories, cognitive science research in reading is increasingly opaque to intuition.

A third reason is Department of Education funding policy. It is my belief that the department has underfunded research into the nature of reading and its acquisition, insisting that priority should be given to studies that seem immediately practical. As a result, research is being left undone that would advance our understanding of fundamental issues, and which often would provide facts and precise concepts to illuminate issues of practice. To be sure, some behavioral scientists doing research on reading receive research grants from other sources, but more and more they see themselves as having little in common with literacy educators; they don't attend reading and writing conferences; they don't mingle with teacher educators or applied researchers, let alone teachers; their writing is impenetrable to most literacy educators; they neither shape nor are they being shaped by the practical field of literacy education. To keep literacy education connected with basic research, the next incarnation of the national reading research center ought to include fundamental scientific research on reading and writing, whatever else it does.

Learning to Read and Write

The most fundamental of all issues in reading are how young children learn to read and write and how best to teach them. Yet, we still do not have a satisfactory, comprehensive account of children's acquisition of literacy. What are needed are microgenetic studies of the incremental changes in children's understanding and skill. The research should aim to reveal the typical progression in the development of literacy, if there is one, or the alternative courses of development. The studies should be designed to reveal how children are influenced by joint participation with adults in early literacy activities, such as listening to and discussing stories and using alphabet books, and, later, how they respond to, and are influenced by, the major components of school reading and writing programs.

Studies should examine the social contexts of early literacy, addressing whether the pattern of development is influenced by the sorts of activities children participate in and the nature of their participation. The studies should pay attention to the detail of how activities proceed, including the roles played by parent and child or teacher and child, the nature of the support offered by the adult, the aspects of the task that are emphasized, and the nature of the child's involvement, in order to determine how these variations may influence development.

It is possible that different kinds of children succeed and fail in different reading and writing programs. Who is at risk in an intensive phonics program? Who in a whole language program? Who in basal programs? The questions should be asked, especially, about children who come from low-literate homes.

All facets of reading and writing should be considered in new studies of early literacy, including influences on children's construction of meaning and their personal responses to literature. However, there is good reason why research and development should give special attention to how children learn to identify words accurately and fluently. Research over the past 15 years reaffirms the central importance of word identification in learning to read and provides new leads about how the process works. Yet, teachers have been getting mixed messages. There are those who claim that the importance of word identification has been exaggerated. Many insist that children can readily discover what they need to know about word identification simply as a byproduct of reading and writing activities. Others maintain that direct instruction in phonics is the best way. The cacophony of voices on early reading has left teachers confused. Therefore, there is a particularly pressing need for clarity on the surest route for children to develop the ability to identify words.

Children in the early grades and even in kindergarten are doing much more writing than they did a decade ago. In addition to being a valuable aspect of literacy in its own right, there are a number of indications that writing promotes reading. Further research should investigate the interrelationships between reading and writing development. Does being engaged in writing promote children's phonemic awareness, spelling, and word identification and, if so, under what conditions? What are the consequences of encouraging invented spellings, and how do these compare to the consequences of expecting conventional spellings?

It is now clear that *phonemic awareness* serves as a crucial part of the foundation for learning to read. Phonemic awareness is the ability to segment words into the sounds that comprise them. Research establishes that children who can hear the sequence of phonemes in spoken words usually learn to read easily; without this ability learning to read an alphabetic language such as English is very difficult. Initial studies have revealed that phonemic awareness can be taught. These studies need to be extended. Early literacy activities need to be examined to determine whether, as typically used, they promote phonemic awareness. New activities to promote phonemic awareness should be designed and evaluated.

A specific issue is what the units of word analysis are for children of different levels of development. Research indicates that adults normally use all of the information available in the letters and associated sounds when identifying words. For a child learning to read, however, initially words may be identified using only partial letter and sound information, perhaps only the first letter and a helpful context. We have incomplete answers to several questions. What aspects of letter and sound information do children at different stages of development use? Does what they use depend on how they are taught? When do they begin to analyze words in terms of useful parts such as roots and affixes and onsets and rimes (e.g., the *t* and *-eam* in team). Which activities and instructional practices promote children's ability to use the information in word parts? A better understanding of the aspects of letter and sound information that children are able to use will be valuable in improving methods for teaching reading.

One of the most urgent research agendas is the education of children from linguistically diverse backgrounds. It is simply not possible to assume that learning to read a second language is the same as learning to read in one's first language. One line of research needs to examine the cognitive processes of bilingual children reading in both their first and their second language. Such within-child comparisons can help answer several questions: What are the specific differences between reading in the one's first and second language? What are the sources of difficulty for reading in the second language? How do skills and knowledge in the first language affect reading in the second language?

The Acquisition of Knowledge

A persistent problem in U.S. education is the difficulty many children have in acquiring knowledge from the written word. This is a problem with multiple causes. Several facets of the problem have been illuminated by research of the past 15 years, but the root causes are in urgent need of further study.

A major cause of difficulty in acquiring knowledge is the poor quality of textbooks. No one who has seriously examined elementary or secondary textbooks has been pleased with what he or she sees. Textbooks often do not present a treatment of a subject matter that is recognizable to practicing members of the discipline. Textbooks speak with the voice of omniscient authority. Seldom is the basis for assertions presented. Seldom are hedges and qualifications included. Textbooks do not explain and justify models in a field of inquiry. What they do is "cover" the subject matter.

Why are textbooks so bad? In the most fundamental terms, the poor quality of textbooks reflects lack of understanding, or misunderstanding, of the nature of knowledge in subject matter disciplines. The improvement of textbooks requires not just more money, or better intentions, but a better understanding of what knowledge in a subject matter looks like, and how this knowledge is acquired.

The picture that emerges from analyses of textbooks is of pages that are densely packed with information, but that explain and illustrate few concepts adequately for young readers. Vast stretches of history, geography, and science are compressed into brief passages. The result is a listlike presentation of disconnected information, as in the following excerpt from a 200-word passage in a middle grade geography textbook that encapsulates 200 years of European exploration, attempted settlement, and take over of the Sahara Desert: "The first European to reach Timbuktu was Rene Caille.... France even wanted to build a railroad across the Sahara.... By the 1900s, almost all the Sahara belonged to European countries" (cited in Beck, McKeown, & Gromoll, 1989, pp. 122–123).

Textbook presentations typically have a flat structure with little differentiation of important and less important information. Asides and digressions may get as much space as what presumably are central ideas. For instance, 40% of a brief section in the same textbook just excerpted, supposedly describing the size, location, and physical features of the Sahara Desert, is actually taken up with a description of the Kalahari Desert and the fact that Sahara means desert in Arabic. For another example, one from a different middle grade textbook, more space in a section entitled "Our Government" is devoted to such information as the thickness of the marble on the Washington Monument (in inches and centimeters) and the dimensions of the East Room of the White House (in feet and meters) than is devoted to the judicial branch of the government.

Explanations in textbooks frequently do not explain very well. The point of an explanation may be obscure. The steps may be in an illogical order. There may be gaps that must be filled by the reader, if the explanation is to make sense. The explanation may contain premises that young readers will find implausible. Before–after, cause–effect, part–whole, or member–set relationships may not be explicitly marked, but left for the reader to infer. Here is a passage from a middle grade science textbook that illustrates several of these shortcomings: "In the evening, the light fades. Photosynthesis slows down. The amount of carbon dioxide in the air spaces builds up again. This buildup of carbon dioxide makes the guard cells relax" (cited in Armbruster, 1984, p. 210).

The following paragraph is a more coherent version of the same content. The rewritten explanation has a point, important steps missing in the original have been included, and relationships among the steps have been clarified:

> What happens to these processes in the evening? The fading light of evening causes photosynthesis to slow down. Respiration, however, does not depend on light and thus continues to produce carbon dioxide. The carbon dioxide in

the air spaces builds up again, which makes the guard cells relax. The relaxing of the guard cells closes the leaf openings. Consequently, leaf openings close in the evening as photosynthesis slows down.

A not insignificant reason for poor textbooks is a misguided standard for what will make a book easy enough for students to comprehend. Publishers and schools rely on readability formulas, according to which a book is readily comprehensible if it possesses two features: It has easy words. It has short sentences. By these criteria the following passage ought to be easy:

The world is all that is the case.
The word is the totality of facts, not of things.
The world is determined by the facts, and by their being all the facts.
For the totality of facts determines what is the case, and also whatever is not the case.
The facts in logical space are the world.
The world divides into facts.
Each item can be the case or not the case while
everything else remains the same.

The foregoing passage is the opening statement from a famous work on logic and philosophy by Ludwig Wittgenstein (1961, p. 7). Most people do not find it easy to understand, despite its uncomplicated syntax and familiar words. In general, easy words and short sentences do not guarantee ease of comprehension. Likewise, complexity of syntax and unfamiliar words are not so much the causes of difficulty in comprehension as they are symptoms that a passage is about a complex, unfamiliar subject.

Trying to make a text more readable by shortening the sentences may actually interfere with comprehension. The *becauses, thens,* and *howevers* are removed and students are left on their own to figure out how propositions relate to one another. "Editing to formula" is one of the reasons that textbooks are filled with choppy, disconnected passages and explanations that do not explain.

That easier words will make a textbook less difficult to understand may seem to be an uncontroversial proposition. Unfamiliar words are always the first obstacle to comprehension that students mention. Still, the proposition is at best a half-truth.

Although readability formulas aim at both shorter sentences and easier words, it is clear that, if one wants to keep the content the same, there is a trade-off between ease of vocabulary and sentence length. To explain the same idea in simpler words will take more space, and usually more complex sentences. The reason is that one technical word represents concepts that it takes many simple words to explain. For example, here is a sentence from a basal reader selection about earthquakes, containing the hard word *geophysicist:* "A third study has been set up along the San Andreas fault, where geophysicist Ruth Simon, who has studied animals and quakes since 1972, has set up cockroaches in three carefully watched stations."

If you wanted to keep the content exactly the same, but use "simpler" words, you could replace the word geophysicist with the definition found in the glossary: "A third study has been set up along the San Andreas fault, where Ruth Simon, a person who applies the laws of physics to the study of the structure of the earth, and who has studied animals and quakes since 1972, has set up cockroaches in three carefully watched stations."

The resulting sentence is 50% longer than the original, and not necessarily easier to understand. Of course, the text could be watered down—the word *scientist* could be used in place of *geophysicist*. Depending on who the students are and the purpose of the instruction, this may be an acceptable substitution in this case, but as a general rule replacing technical words is a step that can end up undermining comprehension.

Technical vocabulary—if rightly explained and rightly used—can make a text easier to understand. How, for instance, can one talk intelligibly about the anatomy of the heart without using the term *ventricle*? Technical vocabulary is itself a component of the content to be learned from textbooks. Students may not need to know the word *combustion* to study combustion, but if they don't learn the meaning of the word *oxygen*, they have not learned very much. In short, when and how to introduce technical vocabulary are matters of great importance to both textbook authors and classroom teachers. Studies of vocabulary must be regarded as foundational in any program of research on the acquisition of knowledge.

A basic problem with the notion that easier words make for easier texts is that the notion of easy words is itself problematical. What makes a word easy or hard is not a simple matter. Readability formulas use word length or word frequency as indices of word difficulty, but neither length nor frequency necessarily make a word hard.

Recent evidence suggests that whether a word is difficult or easy is primarily a function of how difficult a concept it represents. In the passage from Wittgenstein quoted earlier, *space* is an easy word and *logical* is not so hard, either. It is when the two words are combined in the phrase *logical space* that comprehension becomes uncertain. The reason is that *logical space* is an unfamiliar concept to most readers.

Recognizing conceptual difficulty as the major factor underlying vocabulary difficulty is an important step forward. However, it serves largely to uncover the next layer of research questions, rather than to provide immediate practical answers: What types of concepts are especially difficult for students? Are teachers able to determine which words are likely to be conceptually difficult for their students? To what extent is the conceptual difficulty of a word a function of its role in the text? What methods of instruction are especially effective or ineffective for difficult concepts?

A common practice is for the teacher to try to make a technical subject easier by "preteaching" key vocabulary, that is, by introducing selected difficult but important words before students read a textbook chapter. The way this often happens is that students look the words up in a glossary and use each one in a sentence. This is a tedious exercise, and it does not work very well, especially when the student is unsophisticated about words or lacks background knowledge about the topic.

Why is this widespread practice ineffective? One reason is that children are surprisingly inept at learning new meanings from definitions. To illustrate the problem, given the definition of *usurp* as "to seize and hold power, position or authority by force and without right," one child produced the sentence, "He has the usurp to put me in jail." This response is not atypical, and it is evidence of a rather deep misunderstanding of the definition. Can conventions for writing definitions be improved, so that word meanings are made accessible to more young readers? Can instruction in using glossaries and dictionaries be improved, so that young readers will have a better chance of digging the meanings out of definitions? An even more fundamental question is whether study of difficult vocabulary should come first, followed by efforts after conceptual understanding, or whether learning the words and learning the system of concepts should go hand in hand.

There are other important questions about children's vocabulary growth that remain unanswered, or to which the available answers are controversial. Functionally speaking, for children at different levels of development, what is a word? For instance, is there an age at which *loyal, loyalty,* and *disloyal* are treated as entirely distinct words? And, is there a later age at which these words are seen as members of a family, such that as soon as one is known the meanings of the others are easily computed? What are the relative contributions of oral language experience and reading to children's vocabulary growth? What must a child know about the nature of word meanings in order to have a good chance of learning a word upon simply hearing it or reading it in context? Can instruction be designed that will help children become better independent word learners?

Bilingual children often have a limited English vocabulary, and this is no doubt one reason they may experience difficulty learning from textbooks. Most technical vocabulary, however, has a clear morphological structure and roots that are found in many languages. Thus, bilingual children may know cognate words, or words in their first language that are related in form and meaning to the technical vocabulary of English. The extent to which bilingual children notice and use cognates is unexplored territory, which should be examined in future research.

It would not be safe to assume that most teachers are able to overcome the deficiencies of textbooks, so that their students are able to arrive at a deeper and more critical understanding of the subject. In the all too typical classroom, the textbook defines the curriculum. The students plod through the book chapter by chapter. Especially in classes perceived as low in academic ability and motivation, a frequent practice is for students to take turns reading sections from the book aloud. The oral reading is punctuated with recitations over the material just covered. Usually there will be an accompanying written assignment. Successful performance in recitations and on written assignments and examinations typically hinges on having memorized propositions from the book.

Teachers and textbook authors seem to proceed on the assumption that students' minds are blank slates. Yet, the most fundamental insight we have is that learning depends on prior knowledge. More important than particular facts the student knows, or does not know, is the system of concepts that the student will bring to bear. Even when, at first blush, it may seem that students do not know anything relevant about a topic, recent research reveals that they will be applying what have come to be called *naive theories*. A naive theory is a set of ideas students have spontaneously developed to make sense of the world around them, as well as the things adults tell them.

Students' naive theories may be at odds with the approved theories the school champions. Because of commitments to naive theories, students may find explanations couched in terms of approved theories incomprehensible, or they may distort explanations to maintain consistency with a naive theory, or they may compartmentalize—using a version of the approved theory for school work but hanging on to their own theory for life outside of school. The conflict between naive and expert theories has been documented in several areas of science, and no doubt occurs in the humanities and social sciences as well. For instance, from research we know that children whose experience tells them the earth is flat may preserve this belief, and at the same time accommodate the adult information that the earth is round, by supposing that the earth is round like a pancake, instead of round like a ball, or by supposing there are two earths, the flat one we walk around on and the spherical one pictured in science books.

The nature of naive theories, how children come to formulate them, and the conditions under which they will change is an exciting area of inquiry. There are still many unanswered questions that should be pursued vigorously. For educational application, we will need a characterization of naive theories in each area of the curriculum for children of various levels of development. Also required for educational application is an understanding of how students can be led to change their theories. Naive theories have proved amazingly resistant to change. In fact, nothing tried to date has proved especially successful in getting students to abandon naive theories and replace them with expert theories.

So, what sense can be made of the persistent difficulty that many children have in acquiring knowledge from the written word, the poor quality of textbooks, and the superficial quality of much classroom instruction in the sciences, social sciences, and humanities? A complete and confident answer must await more research. In the meantime, it can be said that the problem is almost certainly systemic. Most fundamentally, it reflects beliefs about the nature of knowledge and the nature of learning on the part of those who produce books and those who use them. It reflects the understanding that authors, editors, and publishers have of the task of producing books. It reflects the forces of the market place, the fact that to sell books a company must avoid offending anyone and satisfy the least common denominator of every school's curriculum. It reflects teachers' conceptions of their job, the forces that constrain their work, and the instructional strategies they know how to use. It reflects students' goals, the beliefs they have about what it takes to be successful in school, the concepts they have about what knowledge is, and how they could come to possess it.

An interlocking set of problems requires an interlocking set of research agendas. In addition to the specific questions raised throughout this section, several broad questions should be addressed: What are the deep reasons why a textbook is easy or difficult to understand? How should books be written if they are to promote conceptual understanding? What forces in the writing, editing, and marketing of textbooks vitiate quality? As for the schools, which aspects in the process of reviewing and selecting textbooks mitigate against quality and how can the process be improved? How can conceptual understanding be nurtured in the classroom? What classroom ethos and instructional strategies distinguish successful teachers of the humanities, sciences, and social sciences from the less successful?

Critical Reading and Thinking

Evidence continues to appear that U.S. students do not reason well about written material. We need to find out why and what to do about it.

Educators always give lip service, at least, to inquiry, problem solving, and reasoning. At the same time, descriptions of classroom instruction seldom show much time and attention given to promoting higher order thinking. This contradiction suggests that there must be forces conspiring to prevent higher order thinking goals from being achieved. Research should try to identify what these forces are.

A plausible countervailing force is one realization of a commitment to basic skills. A widespread assumption in education is that skills and knowledge form a hierarchy or pyramid. In the case of reading, skills near the bottom of the pyramid include knowing consonant blends, dividing words into syllables, and finding words in a dictionary. Near the apex are skills such as evaluating the logical consistency of an argument or formulating reasons in defense of a position. If a teacher always starts at the bottom, so to speak, with the lowest level skills students have not yet mastered, higher level skills may get crowded out of the curriculum. Commitment to the notion of a skills hierarchy may explain the finding suggested in some research that high-ability reading groups are allowed to spend more time in intellectually stimulating discussion of texts than low-ability reading groups. Is this apparent difference in the hidden curriculum of reading groups of different levels justifiable in terms of the long-term progress of the children? Or, are children in low groups being short changed?

Another possible explanation for the lack of attention to vigorous and wide-ranging thought is that teachers are constrained by external pressures. One such pressure is to cover the curriculum, defined as completing the textbook and accompanying exercises. Another external pressure, many argue, is the requirement to prepare students to pass school-mandated or state-mandated tests that may not require much thinking. Of course, holding teachers and students accountable for performance on tests is one of the mainstays of the current educational reform movement. It would be a bitter irony if educational reform were to depress the level of thinking in our schools. What skills and abilities do educators assume are required for students to pass various kinds of tests? What do they assume is the best short-term method of preparing for tests? What skills and abilities, in fact, improve performance on various mandated and recommended tests? How does the allocation of time to different activities and the character of classroom discussion change as the result of tests?

A basic problem is that a large number of teachers may not have instructional strategies for cultivating critical thinking. This proposition is probably true in many fields; it is certainly true in the field of reading. In the conventional reading lesson, children discuss a story every day, but typically the discussion is not mind-expanding. It consists of a recitation to make sure that the children have grasped the main points of the story. Beyond this, good teachers lead children in a search for some broader moral implied by the story, but, again, exercise of critical thinking is seldom called for. There simply are not well worked out and widely recognized instructional strategies for promoting critical thinking within the field of reading. Designing, evaluating, and disseminating strategies for enhancing critical reading and thinking ought to be a priority for reading research and development.

The Education of Reading Teachers

The quality of the instruction children receive is a major factor in their rate of growth in reading. Quality of instruction is a category that includes teachers' ability to motivate children and inspire them to read widely, knowledge and skillful use of best available methods and strategies, command of effective teaching techniques, ability to adapt lessons to take account of the needs of individual children, and skill in managing a classroom so as to make it a pleasant and productive place.

Except for children's reading level at the beginning of the year, quality of instruction is perhaps the overriding factor in children's growth in reading during that year. It must be acknowledged that, although this conclusion is sensible, it is hard to prove; it is an inference from such facts as that there usually is a considerable amount of variation in end of year performance among classes ostensibly using the same reading program, after discounting level of performance at the beginning of the year. Research should attempt to pin down the role of quality instruction in children's reading growth.

According to *Becoming a Nation of Readers* (Anderson, Hiebert, Scott, &

Wilkinson, 1985, p. 120), "America will become a nation of readers when the verified practices of the best teachers in the best schools can be introduced throughout the country." Regrettably, research in classrooms has consistently shown that average practice falls considerably short of best practice. Why is this so? The general form of the answer is that teacher education is woefully inadequate and that teachers typically have impoverished opportunities for continuing professional growth and development.

A major shortcoming of teacher education is that it depends too much on lectures and textbooks. Preservice teachers, especially, do not have the experience with children or with teaching to make sense of all this abstract talk. Yet, the solution is not as simple as more involvement in classrooms and extended time in student teaching. The classroom in which a would-be teacher observes may not be exemplary. If it is exemplary, the would-be teacher may miss the features that make it exemplary because he or she does not have trained eyes. Reliance in teacher education on classroom involvement alone might well increase the grip of what has been called "the hand of the past" on the prospective teacher's mind and heart.

A similar problem plagues inservice teacher education. There is an overreliance on brief and superficial workshops. If the method introduced in a workshop is at all complicated, teachers will not have a real opportunity to master it. This is probably one reason that complicated procedures such as reciprocal teaching have proved to have variable effects when evaluated at different sites around the country. In the hands of the pioneers and teachers trained by them, reciprocal teaching produced striking results; the results produced elsewhere were often smaller and sometimes not significant.

Research should attempt to identify the features of successful teacher training programs and the weaknesses of less successful programs. Differences between the two that are likely to be critical are that the former find a way to integrate theory and practice and find a way to provide extensive practice with timely coaching and feedback. For example, the centerpiece of Reading Recovery training is the "behind-the-glass" session in which a teacher conducts a lesson behind a one-way window with a child with whom he or she is working on a regular basis. On the front side of the window, the other teachers-in-training are led by the teacher trainer in a vigorous discussion of the behavior of the child, the moves made by the teacher, the rationale for the teacher's moves, and other moves the teacher might have made. During their training year, Reading Recovery teachers teach four or five behind-the-glass lessons and participate in discussions of 50 or so lessons taught by their fellow teachers.

There is a consensus that Reading Recovery has such a high and consistent success rate because of the quality of its teacher training. This training is rather expensive and it would not be feasible to use the same procedures with teachers instructing groups of children. Still, the principles embodied in Reading Recovery and other successful programs ought to be generalizable. In the place of live behind-the-glass lessons, role playing, "microteaching" with students who are paid volunteers, and extensive use of videotape ought to be examined in research and development projects.

CONCLUSION

During the past 15 years, research has greatly expanded our knowledge about the reading process. It has also encouraged the development of differing and often competing visions of reading instruction. In this chapter, I have described five research and development programs that I believe will further advance our knowledge and educational practice. Although there are many other worthy programs that could be added to this list, those focusing on the nature of reading, on how children learn to read and write, on how knowledge is acquired, on critical reading and thinking, and on the education of reading teachers hold tremendous promise for the future of reading research.

REFERENCES

Anderson, R. C., Hiebert, E. H., Scott, J. A., & Wilkinson, I. A. G. (1985). *Becoming a nation of readers*. Champaign, IL: Center for the Study of Reading.

Armbruster, B. (1984). The problem of inconsiderate text. In G. Duffy, L. Roehler, & J. Mason (Eds.), *Comprehension instruction*. New York: Longman.

Beck, I. L., McKeown, M. G., & Gromoll, E. W. (1989). Learning from social studies text. *Cognition and Instruction, 6*(2), 99–158.

Tharp, R., & Gallimore, R. (1988). *Rousing minds to life: Teaching, learning, and schooling in social context*. New York: Cambridge University Press.

Wittgenstein, L. (1961). *Tractatus logico-philophicus*. London: Routledge & Kegan Paul.

3

Literacy's Future for All Our Children: Where is Research in Reading Comprehension Leading Us?

Elizabeth Sulzby
The University of Michigan

In projecting the research agenda for the decade leading to the year 2000, one feels the tensions of change perhaps more powerfully than a scant 10 years earlier. In this chapter, I recall many of the agendas not yet finished or only brushed over lightly that still need attention—and project others that appear to be drawing us into the next century in a futuristic stance.

This chapter focuses primarily on young children through the elementary school years, but with a life-span developmental perspective. Thus the title, "Literacy's Future for All Our Children..." signals a cry for keeping the doors open to all kinds of reading and writing understandings and endeavors for all children to the greatest extent possible. This title implies the need to keep theoretical perspectives, research designs, and instructional implementations with both a proximal and distal focus: on the child in the immediate context and on the child as he or she may be in the far future as a result of our theory, research, and instruction.

Since the funding in 1976 of the Center for the Study of Reading (Reading Research and Education Center) at the University of Illinois, following extensive planning and establishing of research agendas, the field of reading research has made important advances that have reshaped our thinking about the reading process. This research agenda has made its most profound change by emphasizing reading as a comprehension process. Resulting in part from that research endeavor, reading research has been positively affected by and has contributed to research in the writing process and how readers and writers engage with and create literature. Almost untouched until now has been research on how reading may be changing with newer technologies. One can characterize the current era as one of growth that has led to tensions in the research communities concerned with reading. A brief examination of a few of these tensions may be illustrative.

One tension has been created through numerous calls for broadening our definitions of literacy or literacies. It is ironic that one of the outcomes of having three federally funded research centers all focusing on differing aspects of literacy (reading, writing, and literature) is an increased awareness of the interrelatedness of literacy processes in the learner and of the need for broadened definitions of literacy/literacies within modern cultures. Although this chapter is addressed formally to the research agenda in reading, in actuality it covers an agenda involving writing and literature as well and implies the need for further coordination between the federally funded centers and staffs supporting the three research agendas.

A second tension occurred from another step forward. Reading research has broadened in the research methodologies used in studies. Researchers have shown an increasing awareness of research paradigms from contributing disciplines and research fields in designing studies and interpreting their own research. For instance, the *Handbook of Research on Teaching the English Language Arts* (Flood, Jensen, Lapp, & Squire, 1991) contains chapters on these related disciplines: linguistics, psychology, including child development, anthropology, and literary theory. Certainly other fields and subfields have also made contributions and, more recently, some researchers (see Snow, Barnes, Chandler, Goodman, & Hemphill, 1991) have turned to sociology for methods and concepts to help us understand literacy in social contexts more fully. In research methodologies, the field has encompassed case studies, longitudinal designs, literary theory, historical studies, ethnographic methods, meta-analyses and other types of research synthesis, as well as experimental designs.

Although these two trends, broadened definitions of literacy and broadened research methodologies, have contributed greatly to our understandings, resultant tensions within the research and practice communities challenge the research efforts for the 21st century. Yet a third source of tension has been the research/practice relationship itself. When the Center for the Study of Reading was first funded at the University of Illinois, it would have been fair to capture this relationship as one of guarded hostility, with researchers being stereotyped as bestowing their findings on untheoretical practitioners.

Since the 1980s, there has been a reshifting of these relationships, so that some practitioners are actively taking part in research (e.g., Allen, Clark, Cook, Crane, Fallon, Hoffman, Jennings, & Sours, 1989); many more are active in setting research agendas and exploring their own theoretical orientations; and most expect research to have quite immediate and useable implications. The roles of major research and practice projects—such as Graves' (1983) and his colleagues' work at the University of New Hampshire and the National Writing Project—were instrumental in reshaping the relationships between research and practice. Also important were grass-roots teacher support groups. Yet another major result can be found in the efforts of textbook publishers and their consultants to bring their books in line with research findings and state calls for changes in textbook design and content (e.g., California State Department of Education, 1987; see also Ruth, 1991).

In many ways, this pressure from practitioners to influence and take part in research is positive. We must, however, take care to continue the careful analytical work that research demands. Such analysis often takes more time than practitioners have and more effort than they are able to expend, without relief from their other duties. Collaborating with practice also places demands on researchers that take away from precious time and resources. Research may be stronger in the long run by having researcher-practitioner collaborations, but it may be much more costly. The cost and benefits of this type of research must be carefully considered, both in the long and short terms. Under any circumstances, with or without additional funding, such researcher–practitioner collaborations call for careful re-thinking of research questions, designs, methods, and interpretations.

With these tensions in mind, I have taken a broad look at what has been done in the past and what needs to be done based on these accomplishments, drawing on research studies, research summaries, and on research-based trends in practice. For simplicity, the chapter is divided into two parts of unequal length: (a) research in comprehension, a continuation of the promise of current research and (b) the future: research in comprehension and composition in a technological age. Key research questions follow each subdivision.

COMPREHENSION: CONTINUATION OF THE PROMISE OF CURRENT RESEARCH

During the 1970s and 1980s, we made tremendous progress in moving from viewing reading as a highly mechanical process to viewing reading as a comprehension process and beginning to understand the comprehension process. This achievement is so important that I have subsumed all of the following sections of related research under their relationship to comprehension.

Reading Comprehension, Narrowly Defined

We have come from an era in which there was very little research on either reading comprehension as a process or on instructional strategies that aid in the development of reading comprehension to an era in which there is much agreement on the importance of both. There is broad agreement that good readers (hence, good comprehenders) approach text constructively, with expectations from their prior knowledge and purposes for reading. The reviews of Tierney and Cunningham (1984), Pearson and Fielding (1991), and Flood and Lapp (1991) all summarized research in which reading comprehension has been taught successfully using techniques drawn from findings about the reading processes of successful readers. Such readers are active during reading and they respond to difficulties strategically; they monitor their comprehension and make self-corrections or use fix-up strategies when they are having difficulty.

Reading comprehension instruction has tended to focus on helping all readers become more active as they read, activate background knowledge such as story or expository schemata and knowledge about the specific topic(s) in the reading passage, ask themselves relevant questions, rehearse or summarize, or apply other, more specific strategies (Dole, Duffy, Roehler, & Pearson, 1991; Paris, Lipson, & Wixson, 1983; Pressley, Johnson, Symons, McGoldrick, & Kurita, 1989).

In general, the good reader studies ignored decoding or text difficulty and focused on comprehension strategies. The instructional studies similarly focused almost entirely on comprehension and either ignored difficulties in decoding or controlled text difficulty. These studies placed insufficient attention on differences between reading for different purposes and, instead, have tended to treat each purpose separately: pleasure, information, studying, and so forth.

Other studies (Anderson, 1977; Anderson, Reynolds, Shallert, & Goetz, 1977; Spiro, 1980; Stein & Glenn, 1979; see also Anderson, Heibert, Scott, & Wilkinson, 1985; Anderson & Pearson, 1984) of the comprehension process focused on the nature of the text itself and its relation to the background knowledge of the reader, within a cognitive psychology framework. Whereas more recent research is focusing on the "text" as readers experience it during given transactions, this research was the forerunner of such theories, in showing that texts that fit readers' expectations are easier to comprehend, certain text deviations can cause comprehension problems, and shifting readers' expectations or perspectives prior to reading can differentially effect what they will comprehend and/or remember.

Research needs to continue in both the areas of research in the basic comprehension processes and in comprehension instruction, reflecting broadened definitions of literacy (literacy for purposes including but broader than literacy for schooling or work). It could be argued that research founded in psychology and linguistics is the work that has thus far had the most impact on our understanding of the reading process. Although such research should clearly be continued, it should now have an added emphasis on the individual learner, on individual differences. (As argued here, teachers use their knowledge of individuals to generalize and create teaching/assessment strategies for groups of students and problematic individuals.)

Research Questions:

- What are the variations of comprehension patterns of individual learners in relation to text difficulty, genre, and purpose?
- Within each area of comprehension research, what are the nature of individual differences and individual patterns of development?
- What are appropriate standards for comprehension? By what standards can we say that students have comprehended and to what degree they have comprehended? What does it mean to say a student has "failed to comprehend"?
- What is reading comprehension the comprehension of? This question is elaborated in the section on literature.

Conprehension and Literature

Most of the influential studies of the comprehension process used contrived texts in order to isolate expected effects. Similarly, until recently, instructional text series (basal readers) were highly dependent on specially written or controlled texts rather than trade literature. Such texts were also unrealistically short. Literary critics (see Beach & Hynds, 1991; Rosenblatt, 1985, 1991) criticized both the use of contrived texts and also narrow ideas of how readers respond to texts. Now research, theory, and practice are increasingly addressed to the nature of literature, both as a focus of comprehension and for its long-term effects on the reader/writer. Understanding of comprehension has changed from an examination of recalls to techniques such as think-aloud protocols and reader retrospectives.

Reading researchers are turning their attention increasingly to the notion that comprehension is multifaceted, both cognitive and affective, and can be treated as a transaction between reader and the text. From this view, text does not contain a set message or group of messages nor does the reader completely construct a set or multiple sets of understandings without being constrained by the text or given purposes for reading. Rosenblatt (1991) explained that "reader response theory" can be viewed as a reaction in literacy theory to the New Criticism that called for a close reading of the text to analyze how the author put the text together to create the work of art: "How does a poem mean?"

Rosenblatt (1991) explained that "reader response theories" are a group of theories that treat the reader as active in at least helping to create the text. Within these theories, she places reader-oriented theories, text-oriented theories (including deconstruction), and reader-plus-text oriented theories, including phenomenology and transactional theory, and political theories. Researchers (Martinez & Roser, 1991; see also Galda & Cullinan, 1991) working with young children increasingly used reader response theories as a base from which to view young children's growing appreciation for and awareness of literature, including how it is used in making the transition from emergent to conventional reading and how it affects children's oral and written language usage. These theories are useful for viewing literary interpretation but they place severe challenges on traditional psychological studies using such measures as match between recall and text as evidence of comprehension and on traditional assessment measures in which one answer is viewed as correct. They also offer challenges for how early literacy development is viewed.

The correction posed to reading comprehension research by literary theory leads to at least three clusters of research questions. These questions have been pushed to a higher level of significance by the explosion of literature-based instructional programs in classrooms over the past 4–5 years. I have phrased these questions for the goals of a reading rather than literature center in that the focus is still on the nature of reading comprehension, with the acknowledgment that some researchers have already begun to address some of these issues.

Research Questions:

• What is comprehension the comprehension of? What can we say about the nature of comprehension of literature, in all its forms or genres, with all its purposes, in contrast with texts contrived for instructional purposes? Are there important differences for the reader between what various canons treat as "good" versus "poor" literature? How does comprehension differ when readers read for different purposes?

• It has been argued that good literature can be experienced or comprehended many times from many vantage points. What is the nature of comprehension over multiple readings of a text? How do strategies change over multiple readings? What attracts a reader to multiple readings?

• Many classrooms are now using only trade literature of various genres for reading instruction. Others are using textbooks that have reproduced such literature in anthologies and use instructional programs incorporating other trade literature with such anthologies. These instructional programs encourage class discussion, reaction to, and writing about literature. What is the outcome of a "literate environment" in a classroom for the comprehension, vocabulary, concept, and knowledge development of a given child? Is explicit strategy instruction still necessary or desirable? What is the nature of discourse in a literature-enriched classroom?

• How do teachers' concepts about literacy and learning processes change as they move toward literature-based programs?

• How do teachers who identify themselves as whole language teachers view literature-based programs? How do teachers who identify themselves as skills-based teachers view them? How do these teachers views change over time? What are the social influences on classroom practices for these teachers?

Comprehension, Emergent Literacy, and the Transition to Conventional Literacy

During the 1980s, we learned that young children do not come to formal schooling as empty vessels concerning literacy; they already have quite extensive experience with literacy that is organized as conceptual knowledge (Sulzby & Teale, 1991; Teale & Sulzby, 1986). One issue that keeps floating about in the literature but is unresolved is whether or not children's emergent literacy represents stages similar to Piagetian stages (Ferreiro & Teberosky, 1982), is developmental in some important but less stagelike manner (Sulzby, 1985, 1989), or is merely an accretion of knowledge. Although the latter position is rarely taken explicitly, it appears in studies that acknowledge that children have much knowledge about literacy but then continue to call children "prereaders" and design studies based on conventional principles as if prior knowledge is not important. Policy statements by the National Association for the Education of Young Children (NAEYC, 1985) and the International Reading Association (IRA, 1989) took the stance that young children have different developmental needs but did not formally address the debate about stages.

When we move to studies of comprehension that focus on emergent and beginning readers, we find a disagreement about whether it is possible or profitable to treat comprehension as separable from decoding. For example, Dickinson (1987) and Adams (1990a) both claimed that poor readers, especially at the younger levels, are also poor decoders and that decoding must be mastered for mature comprehension to take place. Both treated emergent literacy research as providing a valuable set of insights into the kind of rich preschool and home environments that help support the beginning reader. Sulzby and Teale (1991) agreed that emergent literacy research provides such insights but suggested that the research provides knowledge about the mutually developing roles of comprehension and decoding. They also pointed to the transition into conventional literacy as a fruitful point in which to investigate these roles.

Adams (1990a, 1990b) treated children who are not yet reading conventionally as "prereaders," and then interpreted phonemic awareness as a necessary but not sufficient precursor of reading. According to Adams, having been read to is a predictor that is related to later reading achievement. In contrast, Sulzby (1985, 1989), treated reading and writing behaviors from infancy forward as legitimate parts of reading and writing development; Sulzby claimed that children develop knowledge of letter–sound relationships (including phonemic awareness), concept of word, and comprehension of written language concurrently and prior to beginning to read conventionally. When the child integrates these three aspects while processing someone else's text in a flexible, strategic fashion, the child is making the transition from emergent to conventional literacy. In this view, the child is showing comprehension of written language prior to this point and at this point.

These two positions fail to connect because of the lack of agreement on when literacy begins and what counts as literacy. Sulzby treated both phonemic awareness and comprehension as equal aspects of reading that lead into conventional reading and treated reading as a continuum from emergent into conventional reading. Adams (1991) regarded reading as beginning only at the point where children are identifying words from print.

Bypassing the issue of when conventional reading is established, Palincsar and Brown (1989) conducted an implementation of comprehension strategies through reciprocal teaching (see also Palincsar, 1986; Palincsar & Brown, 1984) with first-grade, low-income, poor readers. The study was designed such that as a teacher began the teaching routine, he or she read the text to the children. As the children became more efficient at using the comprehension strategies of summarizing, generating questions, clarifying, and predicting, they themselves began to consult the text and clarify from the text at levels not expected by traditional standards of decoding proficiency. Evidently, having a set of strategies and problematic situations led them to act like successful readers, perhaps enabling them to match expectations with print more efficiently.

Sulzby found (Sulzby, 1985; Sulzby & Teale, 1987), in a series of studies, that children who were not yet reading from print nevertheless used the comprehension strategies of prediction, monitoring comprehension, and self-correction when attempting to "read" a favorite storybook from the pictures. Additionally, children who were advanced in emergent literacy used overgeneralizations of "written language-like" patterns from a particular book in recreating the text. The claim is that, for children who have been read to, comprehension for written language develops before conventional reading, alongside phonemic awareness, early decoding, and word recognition strategies.

The growth of Reading Recovery projects and their research bases (Clay, 1991; Deford, Lyons, & Pinnell, 1991) also provided another impetus to consider the role of comprehension in beginning to read conventionally. Reading Recovery was designed by Marie Clay in New Zealand as an intensive tutoring program for school beginners. Reading Recovery was targeted at children with the worst prognosis for reading success. Clay and her colleagues at The Ohio State University and an increasing number of training sites in the United States adapted this program for U.S. use.

Currently, the program provides a full year of closely supervised instruction for teacher-trainers who work with a small number of individual children in tutorial sessions. During the sessions, children read and reread numerous small books.[1] Children are given time to make decisions and to

---

[1] A type of writing—from teacher dictation—is incorporated into Reading Recovery, but it is not the composition of connected discourse. At least one Reading Recovery site in the United States has been careful to supplement this type of writing with ample use of composition in the classrooms from which Reading Recovery students come.

use decoding and comprehension strategies. The teachers model, monitor, and provide feedback in strategy use, fading their support as children show more independent control of strategies. They keep track of children's strategy application through running records that recreate the child's oral reading, including comments. Strategies focus on both decoding and comprehension, and decoding is always checked with a comprehension cross-check (e.g., "Does this word make sense here?") Sessions are conducted in booths with one-way mirrors, behind which other teacher-trainers and teachers in training sit and observe. Teachers in training explain their teaching thoughts and decisions. Observers coach each other, and provide feedback to the teacher they observe teaching a lesson. Teacher-leaders return to local districts to train other Reading Recovery teachers, using a similar method. These teachers then work with children intensively, in a one-to-one basis, commonly in pull-out programs.

Adams (1990a) characterized Reading Recovery as being quite similar to other tutoring programs designed by Chall, the Benchmark School (Gaskins, Gaskins, & Gaskins, 1991), or Aukerman. She failed to point out that Reading Recovery teachers are teaching and monitoring strategy internalization and that the long-term teacher training provided is quite different from that in these other programs.[2]

Theoretically, Clay (1991) articulated the actual goal of Reading Recovery as being to enable children to establish inner control over strategic reading behavior. The operational goal of Reading Recovery instruction in the United States has been to bring children with the least favorable odds of achieving success in classroom reading up to the level of children in the "middle achievement" groups of their respective classrooms. This operational decision appears to have a sociological rather than a cognitive, psychological base: Children in the U.S. "low" groups typically receive different, less, and worse instruction than children in "higher" level groups (Allington, 1983). Many other decisions in U.S. Reading Recovery programs (such as the amount of coordination with classroom instruction) are made locally, as pragmatic decisions.

The books used in Reading Recovery are often described as being authentic texts, but many were written for instructional purposes as simplified texts with predictable, interesting features. Suggestions for gradations of such books are provided and the assumption is made that texts can be ordered in some way to reflect difficulty in relation to children's proficiency. This issue of book difficulty is revisited in the following sections on instructional levels and assessment.

Although Clay's earlier research has been instrumental in focusing attention on the developmental nature of early literacy, it is not clear how or the extent to which Reading Recovery is based on developmental theory. Ferreiro and Teberosky (1982) and Sulzby (1985) would question whether

---

[2]The Benchmark School project, however, may attempt to coordinate phonics instruction as strategy application more closely with classroom practice.

all children at a given point (here, first-grade classrooms) would be responsive to instruction that assumed a conventional model of understanding,
even with careful tutoring.

Research Questions:

* What is the nature of the transition from emergent to conventional
literacy? When does comprehension begin? What does it look like in the
young reader/writer? When can it best be taught as strategic behavior?
What are the roles of oral and silent reading in early reading development?
* Are there "stages" of reading development?
* What is the nature of decoding in context? What knowledge about
decoding comes from encoding (i.e., invented and conventional spelling)?
What aspects of decoding should be taught separately and what should be
taught in context? How does the nature of the classroom instructional
program affect how decoding is instructed?
* What is the relationship between child development and conventional
reading? Previous researchers asked: When and under what circumstances
can young children be taught to read? Now we ask the same question but
with new knowledge about development and the continuum between
emergent and conventional reading. What is the nature of children's development who undergo programs that place them into conventional reading
at a particular time, especially those programs with some basis in developmental principles (such as Reading Recovery)?

Comprehension and Composition

Research in the writing process, or the process of composing connected
discourse, has contributed much to our understanding of readers and their
concepts of texts. Graves (1983) and many others illustrated that young
children go through similar steps in writing as do accomplished, published
authors. Instructional programs in writing have encouraged teachers to
help students become aware of the nature of the writing process and to use
strategies to improve their writing. Such strategies include ways of improving planning through the generation of goals and ideas; getting feedback
for revision from teachers and peers in conferences; and drafting, editing,
and bringing a piece to "publishable" quality. Applebee (1986) criticized
the ways in which this research has often been institutionalized in U.S.
schools. Nevertheless, research on the writing process had a tremendous
impact on instructional approaches to teaching writing in U.S. classrooms.

Research in writing has also led reading researchers to rethink their
models of the reading process to include the relationship(s) between writing and reading. In a brief but influential article, Tierney and Pearson (1983)
suggested the investigation of a composing model of reading, arguing that
each step of the writing process can be paralleled in the reading process of
an active comprehender. The data base for this model consisted of "think-

alouds" by secondary school readers and writers, each showing awareness of the artistry or constraints of the other. From this model, the comprehension process is guided primarily by attempts to make sense of a given text as if it were written by a person intending to make sense. In a study of elementary children's reading and writing across genres, Langer (1986) successfully used a strategy scheme based primarily on the composition process to analyze the reading and writing behaviors of young students.

Across levels of emergent and conventional writing, research in writing assumes that the writer is monitoring text production and possible interpretations. Graves (1983) demonstrated how the use of teacher and peer conferencing can help young writers articulate their intended meanings and effects on readers. Harste, Woodward, and Burke (1984) and Sulzby (1983) described emergent writers composing messages in scribble, drawing, or other nonreadable forms, yet reading back from these forms. Many of these child writers showed clear evidence of planning in pausing, looking reflectively off in space, talking about an intended text, or making self-correction statements.

Research in composition by the young child showed that emergent writers develop from writing nonreadable forms to writing readable forms (Sulzby, 1989). During that development, children write with phonetic or invented spelling. Microgenetic analysis (Sulzby, 1983) of instances of children sounding out during encoding to invented spelling shows children exploring sounds around a phonetic zone that is appropriate, particularly with vowels. In reading, one of the important parts of phonemic awareness is segmenting sounds, then blending them back to word units. Vowels are particularly difficult to blend because their pronunciations vary with the surrounding context.[3] Thus, young readers need a flexible approach to decoding strategies, including checking sound with sense. The writing of connected discourse allows a reader to explore encoding strategies in a meaningful context that is of an appropriate level of difficulty for the composer.

Dyson's research (1988, 1991) illustrated, with elegant ethnographic detail, that even young kindergarten and first-grade children from impoverished backgrounds make rich use of the full range of the writing process and that writing can be part of their social worlds inside the classroom. By social worlds, she includes both academic achievement and standing, their standing among peers, and their self-concepts. Her research did not, however, address directly the nature of children's reading development nor the comprehension process.

We need a much tighter communication between researchers of the writing and reading processes, such as that provided by Tierney (1991) and others whose work he reviewed. As I view it now, reading researchers tend to treat writing too much as a vehicle through which children become more proficient readers. Conversely, writing researchers tend to ignore children's

---

[3]To a lesser extent, consonant pronunciations also vary contextually.

reading development and the research in reading. We need much more research at all age levels that examines the student as developing writer/reader and more discussion of what constitutes development (see Stanovich, 1986).

Research Questions:

- How is the role of comprehension the same or different when one is reading one's own composition, both during composition and after completion, in contrast with reading someone else's text?
- What part of reading instructional time and effort can be replaced by writing instructional time? To what extent can reading and writing instruction be integrated with ecological validity?

Comprehension, Instructional Level, and the Zone of Proximal Development

Several lines of research have led researchers to rethink some old standards in the field of reading and new candidates for replacing them. One of those is the idea of instructional level and its candidate replacement, the zone of proximal development (ZPD; Vygotsky, 1978, 1981). There is, of course, research on both the zone of proximal development and the Informal Reading Inventory. The purpose here is simply to raise the issue of difficulty level of texts in relation to readers in regard to these two concepts.

Instructional level in reading comes from a long line of reading research and practice in the United States. It was popularized in the 1930s and expounded in great detail in 1946 by Emmett Betts in his classic textbook, *Foundations of Reading Instruction*. Betts based his entire reading theory squarely on the notion of readiness in its psychological sense: Any new learning is dependent on the learner's being developmentally ready for the next step. A teacher can only teach that which is slightly above the child's current level of functioning. Readiness incorporates both cognitive and motivational aspects; the learner is alert and attuned to learning next steps. If the step that the teacher tries to teach is too great, students will be frustrated and fail to learn no matter how well the teacher teaches. In addition to having levels at which learning is rather easy and attainable or is out of reach, students also have independent levels at which previous learning has become automatic.

Betts' levels were termed *independent*, *instructional*, and *frustrational*. A fourth level, the *potential level*, encompassed aptitude; it was operationalized as listening comprehension. In Betts (1946), each level was discussed in detail and detailed steps for extensive informal assessment, called an informal reading inventory (IRI), were outlined. In the years that followed, these levels, their operationalization, and interpretations became oversimplified and mechanized to the point where they began to embody features of the highly controlled basal readers of the 1950s to 1970s. Formalized IRIs were designed and sold, with extremely short contrived passages and lists of comprehension and vocabulary questions. The mechanical levels of 95% word recognition and 75% comprehension replaced the sensitive interpretation of a clinically oriented teacher. Betts' original notion was that each of these levels was a psychological space defined by the child's experiencing of "ease" or "frustration" in reading situations.

Betts' ideas were often implemented in a mechanical fashion and it became the fashion to try to fit children into basal readers at their "instructional reading level" as if this were some semisteady state of books and of children. Chall (Chall & Squire, 1991) criticized textbook publishers during the 1960s and 1970s for responding inappropriately by rolling back difficulty levels, particularly vocabulary loads, in basals as well as other textbooks.

This issue of appropriate difficulty levels is far from dead, although current research and theory support providing children with literacy-rich classrooms and experiences, including much reading and rereading of real literature and the composition of meaningful texts. Children in such classrooms are invited to experience books at different difficulty levels at a given time, and teachers are offered strategies to vary their instructional demands in relation to the challenges of given books. Some children begin to read conventionally from complex trade books, yet they occasionally return voluntarily to very simple books, seeming to feel the need to practice the speech to print match (Sulzby, 1989). The books in Reading Recovery are "graded," albeit by a much broader set of criteria for predictability than those of skills-based reading series.

Adams' (1990a) review included a strong defense of the view that proficient readers actually process every word when reading silently for meaning, rather than sampling selectively from the printed page to confirm meaning as she interpreted top-down models of the reading process to assert. In the Adams (1990b) summary, recommendations were made for the inclusion of specially contrived texts controlled for elements from phonic instruction into literacy-rich classrooms, although such texts were not recommended to replace trade literature.

With the trend toward instructional rubrics such as literature-based instruction, literacy-rich environments, whole language, process writing, authentic assessment, and so on, the IRI has fallen into further disrepute or questionable status. Goodman's (1967) and his colleagues' research in the nature of children's oral reading and retelling was particularly influential in drawing researchers' and teachers' attention to the knowledge, rather than lack of knowledge, to be observed in children's oral reading errors, or miscues. It is now fairly well established that students can read texts in which they make many miscues if they are interested in the topic or if the text ideas are highly predictable. Predictability itself appears to vary across many yet to be investigated dimensions, as well as those that have been explored. By focusing on children's strengths, Reading Miscue Inventory (RMI) techniques remind us that children do not "have" one instructional level, defined by some one or two criteria such as word frequency or sentence length. Yet, we can still distinguish sets of books likely to be appropriate for a given age or developmental level. Teachers are often left with conflicting statements from the research community about how to select books most appropriate for their children.

A candidate for replacement of the notion of instructional level from the IRI is Vygotsky's idea of the ZPD. The ZPD is conceived as a psychological space between the level at which the student can perform a task independently and the level at which he/she cannot perform it even with help. Between those levels, students can solve problems, comprehend texts, compose passages, and build models with the scaffolding of a caring adult. The role for the teacher, then, is to help support the student in performing a role, function, or task that he or she cannot do alone. It appears that the ZPD notion returns us somewhat more closely to Betts' original concepts for IRI levels.

This whole set of ideas moves us into a set of issues involving the nature of what counts as reading and what counts as reading instruction. In Flood and Lapp's (1991) review of reading instruction research, they recounted what appears to be a somewhat esoteric argument about whether comprehension should be taught. Carver's (1987) argument was that much of what is taught under the name of comprehension is actually study skills that enable students to take more information from difficult materials. He asserted, however, that simple practice in reading materials at the instructional level would do a better job. Lapp and Flood concluded that the counter evidence (Haller, Child, & Walberg, 1988), although presenting a convincing argument that comprehension can be taught, was, nevertheless, based on a different definition of comprehension.[4] In spite of his skepticism, Carver (1987) cited as the work that he found most convincing studies by Palincsar and Brown (1984), framed around the issue of the ZPD: Children were scaffolded into using comprehension strategies that they were not yet using voluntarily and then supported until there was evidence that they had internalized these strategies.

Vygotsky's (1978, 1981) notion that learning becomes internalized as a result of dialogues between a less experienced and more experienced learner appears to be highly important but not yet sufficiently explored in the field of reading instruction and development. The area of early literacy is an example. Much of the research using the ZPD assumes that the adult will be trying to help the child perform the task conventionally. Bruner's

---

[4]Carver's definition of reading is far more narrowly drawn than the definition used by proponents of whole language, literature-based instruction, or writing and reading connections. It is also far more narrow than the definition used by researchers who study reading in subject matter areas, which would include study skills.

(1978) research and much of the work in parent–child interaction in emergent literacy (Sulzby & Teale, 1991) used the premise that the adult holds a model of child development and then adjusts the instructional demands in terms of the performance that is expected from a young child at this point in development. As studies by Edwards (1989) and Heath (1983) showed, parents do not always hold a useful model of their own child's development and, consequently, communication breaks down. Instruction in what is expected of young children appears to facilitate parents' role in traversing the ZPD.

In the work of Palincsar and Brown (1984, 1989), teachers were taught how to gauge children's levels of proficient processing of texts. Children were allowed to apply strategies independently and were then given feedback. Children were not allowed to be frustrated by text demands. Still, in later work with first graders (Palincsar & Brown, 1989), the emphasis was on students' ability to learn from text rather than on their underlying concepts about reading.[5]

The work in Reading Recovery can, similarly, be conceived as scaffolding along the lines of the ZPD. Reading Recovery teachers carefully assess the child's level of functioning and independent application of strategies. When strategies are not applied that have been taught, students are reminded. If new strategies are needed, they are modeled. However, difficulty levels of texts are carefully monitored in Reading Recovery.

In the 1980s, we came to treat the learner as active in his or her own development, as capable of higher levels of thinking/learning than previously thought possible, and as needing rich instructional contexts for learning. Still, we do not have sufficient information about the relationship between the difficulty level of text and children's development. Similarly, we do not have enough information about the relationship between what children can learn through independent reading in supportive literacy contexts and how much direct instruction is needed if the entire literacy context is enriched.

Clearly, this issue also falls under the umbrella of assessment. Assessment and testing ("Themed Issue," 1989) are burning issues but not within the scope of this discussion.

Research Questions:

- What is the nature of "instructional level" in reading?
- To what extent is teacher support needed to help students comprehend texts? Does instruction above the traditional idea of "instructional level" result in a permanent improvement in students' ability to read material independently?

---

[5]Based on the work of Ferreiro and Teberosky (1982), it would be useful to know if these children came to hold conventional concepts about literacy and were truly conventional readers as a result of the instructional method.

Comprehension, Teacher Development, and What Counts as Instruction

Just as child development has become more important as a topic for research, so has teacher development. Many issues are relevant that cannot be discussed here, such as the composition of teaching staffs by age, experience, background, teaching situation, and so on. Most important is how individual teachers come to internalize newer concepts about literacy and instruction. Teachers are now viewed as being active participants in their own learning, just as children are. Learning about complex topics is viewed as taking time and effort by adult learners (Guskey, 1986; Wood, McQuarrie, & Thompson, 1982). Richardson, Anders, and their colleagues (Anders & Richardson, 1991; Richardson & Anders, 1991; Richardson, Anders, Tidwell, & Lloyd, 1991; see also McCaleb, Borko, Arends, Garner, & Mauro, 1987; Wildman & Niles, 1987) found that teachers hold internal concepts about instruction against which newer ideas are tested. Although there are many influences on when particular new ideas become accepted by teachers, the test is one of practice and not of theoretical presentation or logical argument. Guskey (1986) suggested that a powerful influence in this practical test is whether or not teachers can see the effects on their own students of ideas that were put forward by researchers or other experts.

Three notions are important here: (a) Teacher practice takes place within a theoretical orientation but it may not be one that involves reading or the same theory of reading as that of the researcher; (b) meaningful teacher change is conceptual in nature and takes time; and (c) teachers' knowledge of children and development is crucial. Most teachers who are teaching now went through inservice education without opportunities to work closely with individual children and prior to the time that information such as that reviewed in this volume was available. Until recently, most inservice education for teachers was "one-shot" in nature, brief, offered late in a workday, and separated from practice. The research in teacher development that is encouraging is longitudinal in nature, situated in teachers' classrooms, involves teachers applying ideas with their own students, grows from felt needs of teachers, and involves much discussion with peers. Examples of this type of research that involves opportunities to try out ideas in practice over time and discuss them with colleagues and experts include the Richardson and Anders research cited in this section and the work of Palincsar and Brown (1989; Palincsar & Klenk, 1992). The research in Reading Recovery (Clay, 1991; Deford, Lyons, & Pinnell, 1991) particularly focused on giving teachers longitudinal experience in taking close looks at individual children.

Another relevant line of research includes the work of Dahl and her associates (Dahl & Freppon, 1989; Dahl, Purcell-Gates, & McIntyre, 1989; Freppon & Dahl, 1991). Purcell-Gates and Dahl investigated how individual low-income children experienced instruction on a day-to-day basis in traditional (skills) classrooms. Dahl and Freppon replicated this design with low-income children in whole language classrooms. Using ethnographic techniques, they first verified that teachers were implementing the models that they espoused. They found, particularly with the whole language teachers, that teachers initiated discussions about their own professional growth and application of ideas in teaching during the period of the longitudinal study. Whereas their focus was primarily on the sense that children made of the instruction, the study provided evidence of teacher change over time. Many other researchers reported, both formally and informally, the importance of teacher change during the conduct of studies that focus formally on children.

There is open debate about whether or not instruction must be explicit and is something teachers "do to" children (see the previous discussion about whether comprehension can or should be taught). Often hidden behind this issue is the implicit assumption by researchers and teachers that if teachers are not delivering content in some quite obvious fashion, that they are not teaching. In this regard, early childhood teacher and teachers of older students often differ. Research in emergent literacy (Adams, 1990a; Sulzby & Teale, 1991; Teale & Sulzby, 1986) provided evidence that young children acquire much knowledge about literacy without formal schooling but within supportive contexts in which adults—typically—do a lot of indirect instructing and facilitating (see Canterford, 1991). Research in literature-based instruction and the writing process across elementary and secondary school appear to be rich territory in which to study the relationship between teaching that is facilitative and indirect and that which is facilitative and direct. We need to understand teachers' concepts of what counts as instruction (e.g., is it instruction when teachers are standing and observing students in a carefully selected set of activities?), the degrees to which students need direct instruction as opposed to opportunities to work together and independently, and individual differences in children's needs for direct and indirect instruction.

Research Questions:

- What do we know or what can we learn about teacher thinking and development that will enable teachers to make use of appropriate techniques and theories of reading comprehension and literacy development?
- Do teachers incorporate ideas from close viewing of individual children's development into their classroom practice? If so, how does this work and what can we do to facilitate it?

Comprehension, Contexts, and Children at Greatest Risk

This section addresses two institutions within which comprehension and comprehension instruction takes place—the home and the school. It is assumed that literacy is not one entity, but that it differs across cultures, even within a society. Within home and school contexts, the primary focus of this review is children who are at greatest risk for experiencing difficulty in school. Although any individual child may be at risk of difficulty, the groups at greatest risk tend to be poor, from minority backgrounds, particularly African American. They may have been abused or neglected in some way; they may be from homes in which literacy levels are low or from large urban settings. Increasingly, they may be poor and rural.

Understanding how literacy instruction can be successful with children who have these kinds of risk factors in their backgrounds is of utmost importance. Definitions of success need to be built upon near and far goals that are compatible. That is, successful must be defined not as immediate improvement in standardized test scores, ignoring that immediate improvement might result in a narrowed definition of literacy in the child's adult life. It must not be defined as useful in the long-term but resulting in a miserable life in first or third grade. Work such as Heath's (1983) is an example of a start in this direction. Although her work ended at the elementary school level, she traced children who were "successful" at entry into school but who began to falter at third or fourth grade; similarly, she found other children who showed skills and strategies that would have been useful at third or fourth grade but who were closed out of instruction at the entry level due to a mismatch between their knowledge and the school's demands. We need more analytic work of this sort, extending across the life span. This means that longitudinal work starting at preschool or kindergarten is not only needed but also should be coordinated across the best research teams in the nation, drawing upon diverse groups such as life-span developmental psychologists as well as literacy experts, or sociologists as well as sociolinguists.

In other examples from research in emergent literacy, researchers focused on family life. Teale and Sulzby (1986; Sulzby & Teale, 1991) showed that facilitative parent-child interaction teaches children how to be literate, in ways that support children's development and fit with the expectations of so-called mainstream schooling. Edward's (1989) and Heath's (1984) research found that some parents need to be taught how to scaffold their reading with children in ways that keep children engaged, that are attuned to children's responses, and that move forward with children's increased levels of responding.

Facilitative parenting around literacy is not limited to middle and upper socioeconomic status (SES) families, however. Taylor and Dorsey-Gaines (1988) provided case studies of extremely low SES African-American families in New Jersey that raised successful readers, even during periods of homelessness. Clark (1983), in an ethnographic study of successful versus failing African-American high school students and their families, found a large-scale scaffolding of expectations across time in the families of the successful students. Families kept control of their children but gradually released control as children showed more and more ability.

Gadsden (1990) took a life-span perspective in interviewing people from four generations of African-American families in a small southern town. She found that each generation, from slavery forward, had rich ideas of the forms, functions, and uses of literacy but that literacy changed across generations.

Edwards', Heath's, and Gadsden's research projects appear to have important implications for studies of intergenerational literacy. Across the United States, programs for illiterate adults and/or adults completing high school through alternative routes, such as gaining the GED through Adult Basic Education, are being combined with programs for young preschoolers. These intergenerational literacy programs (Jongsma, 1990; Nickse, 1989; Potts & Popp, 1991) included literacy instruction of various levels for the adults, preschool experiences for the children, and parenting training in sessions where parents work with their small children. These parenting sessions often come to focus on reading to children and/or joint use of computers, often with literacy software programs (Potts & Popp, 1991).

Research in this area could involve parents' initial concepts of literacy and literacy-related parenting and the effects of interventions such as those designed by Edwards (1989). Just as with studies of teacher change, if we expect conceptual change—change that will be permanent—with parents, we should expect it to take time, need demonstration, the opportunity to practice, and opportunities to talk ideas over. Indeed, comparisons of teacher and parental change in concepts of literacy would be extremely interesting because both parents and most teachers have experiences of literacy within parenting situations.

In spite of encouraging results from some studies of interventions in parenting around literacy and information from some studies of home literacy (Teale, 1986), we know little about literacy in homes where risk factors are greatest and children are not doing well. In order to understand what enables some children to be resilient in terms of schooling, we need to understand the contrast group from an equally intimate look—the home. It may be that there are some stresses on the home, on parenting, and on children within homes that call for extraordinary efforts in literacy instruction, if children are to gain the same opportunities to comprehend and write that other children have. If such extraordinary efforts are called for, we need also to be in position to recommend which interventions are most promising in keeping the doors of literacy open for all levels of achievement rather than merely for low-level employment and survival skills.

The second major context for literacy is the school. Many researchers have begun to take a much more contextual or ecological approach to interpreting research designs, implementations, and findings in general than in the past. This approach is particularly critical for research in schools. Prior to the great paradigm wars of the past decades, traditional researchers reported effects of implementing research techniques without describing and being sensitive to the previously existing context. We are still relatively insensitive to describing the reverberations of change that our research involvements bring to classrooms and schools and the counter reverberations of change within schools and districts that further transform research designs.

General intervention research efforts aimed at schools for low-income and minority students (see Comer, 1989; Karweit, 1989; Levin, 1987; Slavin, Karweit, & Madden, 1989) showed some positive effects. Ethnographic studies of such efforts in light of current research in literacy development would be enlightening. Research either studying interventions done by others or mounting interventions themselves need to involve a more systemic approach to the organization of schools. Changing literacy instruction during time slots reserved for literacy may change the time allowed for instruction in other areas, or it may bring about restructuring so that literacy and other curricular areas are combined. Changes in other curricular areas may have unintended effects on literacy instruction. Multiple demands on teachers' time may affect how ready they are to incorporate new ideas into their teaching repertoires that have nothing to do with the validity of the ideas under other circumstances. In schools with large numbers of children with high-risk factors, many of these systemic effects appear to interact negatively so that interventions may have to change in intensity, in time span, or character. We will know little about these interactions unless time and resources are committed to do research with those in greatest need. Conversely, learning more about how such children learn and improve in literacy may have positive effects on the instruction of all our children.

Research Questions:

- What is the nature of direct and indirect literacy instruction in homes, across age levels and groups?
- What are the concepts of literacy embodied in schoolwide interventions for at-risk children that are focused on broad range improvements in student achievement?
- What are the systemic effects and countereffects when literacy interventions are mounted?
- What are the most appropriate interventions for children at greatest risk of school difficulty, across ages and in different contexts?

The previous section assumed that most of literacy is found in published books and children's writings on paper with pencil, paper, or word processed form. Such reading material and written texts tend to be viewed as linear materials on a flat surface, even though a reader may approach them in a nonlinear fashion. The technologies of pencil and printing press are being transformed by electronic media. In the next brief and speculative section, I sketch in some of the challenges to reading research from modern electronic media.

THE FUTURE: RESEARCH IN COMPREHENSION AND COMPOSITION IN A TECHNOLOGICAL AGE

The future is here. Although computers and other technology often fail to live up to science fiction-fed expectations, their rapid infusion into modern culture is amazing. They are rapidly becoming "invisible," in the sense of being totally expected, unmarked rather than unmarked phenomena.

In the introduction to this chapter, I mentioned broadening concepts of literacy. One can become quite esoteric in discussing what literacy can mean in any one society, within any one portion of literacy (see types of literacy criticism in the section on comprehension and literacy aforementioned), or across languages and cultures. Day-to-day modern life, however, brings the esoteric into immediate attention. A sign of broadening forces on literacy became vividly visible in the first moments of awareness of the 1991 war in the Persian Gulf. Most of us were captives in front of television as the screen filled with footage sent via satellites from the battle fronts. Although these scenes were often labeled as "live," they had already been viewed in some fashion long enough for producers to interject computer-generated titles and cautions on the same screen. On the electronic screen, we saw missiles guided by computer technology similar to that which powers our micro-computers. To bring this hidden technology to life for viewers, television producers showed footage of some of the radar screens and computer controls, some of which had been simulated or reproduced for viewing purposes. The fax machine was highlighted in the Persian Gulf (as it had been in Tienenman Square) as a source of communication for "ordinary people" and enlisted personnel, as well as for the press corps and military leaders.

The 1980s brought an almost overwhelming explosion of technology for the general population and for schools. Although computer usage in schools for such usages as word processing and drill continues as an active topic for research in literacy (e.g., Bruce, 1991; Diaute, 1985; Dickinson, 1986; Olson & Sulzby, 1991), other media have often been treated as unrelated to literacy. A notable exception at the elementary school level is the work of Bransford and his colleagues (Bransford, Kinzer, Risko, Rowe, & Vye, 1989) in which the computer is used in a multimedia instructional design to access videotaped material through videodisc format. Such a format allows the students rapid access to material to view and review, much as one would reread a book. This research team views the videodisc version of a given work ("The Young Sherlock Holmes" in the recent study) as having superior properties to a bound book for certain instructional purposes such as learning complex ideas and vocabulary and motivating at-risk learners. The team is applying ethnographic techniques to attempt to understand the complexity of classroom interactions as well as the effects of the program on individual children and teachers.

We need research using broadened ideas of literacy to study the interre-

latedness and differences of video and printed texts. We also need to
examine the new kinds of texts that are being created on computer screens.
A number of software companies are creating "storybooks on screen"
without evidence that children will like such a format or what the effects
will be. Other "texts" have properties such as hierarchical display of
information via embedded "windows." Many of these computer texts have
portions that activate audio and video enactments, so the boundaries
between standard orthography and other forms of representation become
blurry.

With the advent of modern electronic media, many expensive and
complex features of text production have become usable and affordable to
a greater percentage of the population and expected by even more, through
programs such as desktop publishing. Issues of legibility that were topics
of hot research debate in the early part of the 20th century are reemerging
in the 21st. Waller (1991) raised issues such as the roles of graphics to text,
of textual display through columns and sidebars, and of font sizes in the
new *Handbook of Reading Research*. These features are made more immediately usable to a composer through computer technology and more
expected by readers. As Kozma (1991; see also Solomon, Perkins, & Globerson, 1991) pointed out, there is an interplay between the expectations from
movies and television and the expectations of older forms of textual
display.

Even young children from impoverished homes are coming to schools
now with previous experience with technology, including computers.
Whereas videogames contain some traditional literacy (directions, comments by characters in the games, etc.), more important may be ideas that
at first seem farfetched as literacy. Videotapes, computer games, and home
videotape and videodisc players embody the concept of "permanence" that
has often been applied to written literacy. If a video sequence is not
understood, young children quickly learn that they can replay and "see it
again, Sam." Some of the features that have been attributed to complex
literature can also be applied to movies on video; viewers can have more
and more complex or different understandings with different viewings.

Another feature that has been attributed to written literacy is its ability
to capture the imagination of readers. Writers of novels, for instance, may
attempt to evoke an image in their readers of a setting; readers use inferenc-
ing and imaging to recreate what they think the writer is writing about.
New multimedia document design programs are now available on computer that enable the writer to insert a video scene in place of or to embellish
a description. In scientific arenas, computers are being used to allow
students to explore environments that are actually far distant or imaginary.
We do not know the effects on comprehension of these kinds of substitu-
tions.

Computers and other technology are beginning to be called *tools*, including *literacy tools*. As parts of human evolution and endeavor, the term *tool*

has held a privileged status. Tools can be very simple and powered by hand or brute force; they can be machines; or they can simply be the tools of a trade or status, the implements people normally use. We frequently speak of books and pencils as being tools in the sense of implements to do things, to manipulate, communicate, or embody thoughts. We are at an era of seeing the rapid development of a set of tools that are changing human lives—just as other tools, including the pencil or printing press, did in the past.

Although in schools we often see meager examples of technology, schools too are becoming heavily infused with today's technology, either directly or indirectly. Even children with the lowest achievement scores, labeled *at-risk*, have concepts about technology prior to formal schooling, just as they have concepts about traditional literacy. The concentrations of such children in low-income districts, unfortunately, often have fewer and less advanced computers and software than children in more affluent districts. Thus, they tend to have a reduced chance of learning and enjoying computers in the near point and a componentially diminished chance of using them in the far point, as they become adults. Certainly, a large policy issue is who has access to which kinds of technology and, once the technology is within classrooms, who is allowed use it. An important research issue for a reading/literacy agenda is what the effects are of having access and control of technology.

Of course, a key component in the effects of electronic media in the classroom is the classroom teacher. Whereas researchers of computer usage have pointed to the reluctance of many teachers to use computers effectively in classrooms, other researchers (Bransford et al., 1989; Olson & Sulzby, 1991) have used computers longitudinally with classroom teachers, exploring how computers fit into their literacy curricula and into their school day. The issues are complex ones, with pressures for traditional curriculum contents, new societally derived needs of children, and the complexity of new learning that technology brings to teachers. We need to include the development of teachers' knowledge about and use of computers and other electronic media in our agenda entering the 21st century.

Research Questions:

• What is the nature of comprehension of information presented graphically as pictures rather than words?

• What is the nature of comprehension of materials viewed repeatedly? What are the similarities and differences of repeated "readings" of printed stories and articles and videotaped materials.

• What is the nature of composition across media (when writers can insert video segments, music segments, animated cartoons, etc., into a document created on computer)? What is the nature of comprehension of such multimedia compositions?

• What are children's immediate uses and understandings of computer technology? How do these differ across groups of children, particularly low income, urban, rural, and minority children in contrast with more advantaged children? How does immediate access affect later usage of computers?

• What theories can and should guide software development; hardware and software usage; teacher involvement in computers?

CONCLUSION

In the previous discussion of important issues for the reading research agenda, I raised many questions. Most of the issues are continuations of the gains in knowledge about comprehension of the 1970s and 1980s; a few are quite new. All are keyed around a concern that we address issues for those students at greatest need so that we can improve instruction for all our children. A theme throughout the discussion is the need for research to keep in mind the present or near needs of children and the distal or long-term needs of children.

Let us revisit the three tensions from the beginning of the chapter in terms of the final section on the challenges of electronic media in the reading research agenda of the future. The first tension, broadened definitions of literacy, is immediately apparent. We appear to be entering an era in which the way that meanings are represented for users is changing rapidly, both for comprehenders and composers. Previous definitions of "written language" are coming into question. The second tension, with broader methodologies coming from many more disciplinary fields, is also clearly evident. We tended to ignore software development or treat it as atheoretical, yet software has great power to define the literacies that children experience. Finally, the tensions that arise in researcher-teacher collaborations, particularly those of time and monetary costs, become extreme as we consider research agendas that involve electronic media. Just as these tensions accompanied great excitement and change in the research agendas and in practice arenas during the 1970s and 1980s, they are now accompanying research challenges from technological revolution as we enter the 21st century.

REFERENCES

Adams, M. J. (1990a). *Beginning to read: Thinking and learning about print*. Cambridge, MA: MIT Press.
Adams, M. J. (1990b). *Beginning to read: Thinking and learning about print, a summary*. (Summary prepared by S. A. Stahl, J. Osborn, & F. Lehr) Urbana-Champaign, IL: Center for the Study of Reading.

Allen, J. B., Clark, W., Cook, M., Crane, P., Fallon, I., Hoffman, L., Jennings, K. S., & Sours, M. A. (1989). Reading and writing development in whole language kindergartens. In J. Mason (Ed.), *Reading and writing connections* (pp. 121–146). Needham Heights, MA: Allyn & Bacon.

Allington, R. L. (1983). The reading instruction provided readers of differing reading abilities. *Elementary School Journal, 83,* 548–559.

Anders, P., & Richardson, V. (1991). Research directions: Staff development that empowers teachers' reflection and enhances instruction. *Language Arts, 68,* 316–321.

Anderson, R. C. (1977). The notion of schemata and the educational enterprise. In R.C. Anderson, R.J. Spiro, & W. E. Montague (Eds.), *Schooling and the acquisition of knowledge* (pp. 415–431). Hillsdale, NJ: Lawrence Erlbaum Associates.

Anderson, R. C., Heibert, E. H., Scott, J. A., & Wilkinson, I. A. G. (1985). *Becoming a nation of readers: The report of the commission on reading.* Washington, DC: National Institute of Education.

Anderson, R. C., & Pearson, P. D. (1984). A schema-theoretic view of basic processes in reading. In P. D. Pearson (Eds.), *Handbook of reading research* (Vol. 1, pp. 255–292). New York: Longman.

Anderson, R. C., Reynolds, R. E., Shallert, D. L., & Goetz, E. T. (1977). Frameworks for comprehending discourse. *American Educational Research Journal, 14,* 367–392.

Applebee, A. N. (1986). Problems in process approaches: Toward a reconceptualization of process instruction. In A. Petrosky & D. Bartholomae (Eds.), *The teaching of writing, 85th NSSE Yearbook, Part 2.* Urbana, IL: NCTE.

Beach, R., & Hynds, S. (1991). Research on response to literature. In R. Barr, M. L. Kamil, P. Mosenthal, & P. D. Pearson (Eds.), *Handbook of reading research (Vol. 2,* pp. 453–489). New York: Longman.

Betts, E. A. (1946). *Foundations of reading instruction: With emphasis on differentiated guidance.* New York: American Book Company.

Bransford, J., Kinzer, C., Risko, V., Rowe, D., & Vye, N. (1989). Designing invitations to thinking: Some initial thoughts. *Thirty-eighth Yearbook of the National Reading Conference, 38,* 35–54.

Bruce, B. (1991). *Roles for computers in teaching the English language arts.* In J. Flood, J. Jensen, D. Lapp, & J. R. Squire (Eds.), *The handbook of research in the teaching of the English language arts* (pp. 536–548). New York: Macmillan.

Bruner, J. S. (1978). The role of dialogue in language acquisition. In A. Sinclair, R. J. Jarvella, & J. M. Levelt (Eds.), *The child's conception of language* (pp. 241–256). Berlin: Springer-Verlag.

California State Department of Education. (1987). *English language-arts framework for California public schools.* Sacramento, CA: Author.

Canterford, B. N. (1991). The "new" teacher: Participant and facilitator. *Language Arts, 68,* 286–291.

Carver, R. (1987). Should reading comprehension skills be taught? In J. E. Readence & R. S. Baldwin (Eds.), *Research in literacy: Merging perspectives. Thirty-sixth Yearbook of the National Reading Conference.* Rochester, NY: National Reading Conference.

Chall, J. S., & Squire, J. R. (1991). The publishing industry and textbooks. In R. Barr, M.L. Kamil, P. Mosenthal, & P.D. Pearson (Eds.), *Handbook of reading research* (Vol. 2, pp. 120–146). New York: Longman.

Clark, R. (1983). *Family life and school achievement: Why poor black children succeed or fail.* Chicago: University of Chicago Press.

Clay, M. M. (1991). *Becoming literate: The construction of inner control.* Portsmouth, NH: Heinemann.

Comer, J. P. (1989). The school development program: A psychosocial model of school intervention. In G. L. Berry, J. K. Asamen (Eds.), *Black students: Psychosocial issues and academic achievement* (pp. 264–285). Newbury Park, CA: Sage.

Dahl, K. L., & Freppon, P. A. (1989). *Making sense of reading and writing in whole language classrooms: An analysis of knowledge construction by low-SES urban children in kindergarten and first grade* (Proposal [funded] to the Office of Educational Research and Innovation [OERI]). Cincinnati: University of Cincinnati.

Dahl, K. L., Purcell-Gates, V., & McIntyre, E. (1989, June). *Ways that inner-city children make sense of traditional reading and writing instruction in the early grades* (Final report to the Office of Educational Research and Improvement [OERI-G008720229]). Cincinnati: University of Cincinnati.

Deford, D. E., Lyons, C., & Pinnell, G. S. (1991). *Bridges to literacy: Learning from Reading Recovery.* Portsmouth, NH: Heinemann.

Diaute, D. (1985). *Writing and computers.* Reading, MA: Addison-Wesley.

Dickinson, D. K. (1986). Cooperation, collaboration, and a computer: Integrating a computer into a first–second grade writing program. *Research in the Teaching of English, 20,* 141–159.

Dickinson, D. K. (1987). Oral language, literacy skills, and response to literature. In J. R. Squire (Ed.), *The dynamics of language learning: Research in reading and English* (pp. 147–183). Urbana, IL: National Conference on Research in English.

Dole, J. A., Duffy, G. G., Roehler, L. R., & Pearson, P. D. (1991). Moving from the old to the new: Research on reading comprehension instruction. *Review of Educational Research, 61,* 239–264.

Dyson, A. H. (1988). Negotiating among multiple worlds: The space/time dimensions of young children's composing. *Research in the Teaching of English, 22*(4), 355–390.

Dyson, A. H. (1991). *Early literacy development and popular culture.* Paper presented at the meeting of the International Reading Association, Las Vegas.

Edwards, P. A. (1989). Supporting lower SES mothers' attempts to provide scaffolding for book reading. In J. B. Allen & J. M. Mason (Eds.), *Risk makers, risk takers, risk breakers: Reducing the risks for young literacy learners.* Portsmouth, NH: Heinemann.

Ferreiro, E., & Teberosky, A. (1982). *Literacy before schooling.* Exeter, NH: Heinemann.

Flood, J., Jensen, J., Lapp, D., & Squire, J. R. (Eds.). (1991). *The handbook of research in the teaching of the English language arts.* New York: Macmillan.

Flood, J., & Lapp, D. (1991). Reading comprehension instruction. In J. Flood, J. Jensen, D. Lapp, & J. R. Squire (Eds.), *The handbook of research in the teaching of the English language arts* (pp. 732–742). New York: Macmillan.

Freppon, P. A., & Dahl, K. L. (1991). Learning about phonics in a whole language classroom. *Language Arts, 68,* 190–197.

Gadsden, V. L. (1990, December). *Interpretations of literacy by African-American youth and adults: Life-span perspectives.* Paper presented at the 40th Annual National Reading Conference, Miami Beach.

Galda, E., & Cullinan, B. E. (1991). Literature for literacy: What research says about the benefits of using trade books in the classroom. In J. Flood, J. M. Jensen, D. Lapp, & J. R. Squire (Eds.), *Handbook of research on teaching the English language arts* (pp. 529–535). New York: Macmillan.

Gaskins, R. W., Gaskins, J. C., & Gaskins, I. W. (1991). A decoding program for poor readers— and the rest of the class, too! *Language Arts, 68,* 213–225.

Goodman, K. S. (1967). Reading: A psycholinguistic guessing game. *Journal of the Reading Specialist, 6*(4), 126–135.

Graves, D. (1983) *Writing: Teachers and children at work.* Exeter, NH: Heinemann.

Guskey, T. R. (1986). Staff development and the process of teacher change. *Educational Researcher, 15,* 5–12.

Haller, E. P., Child, D. A., & Walberg, H. J. (1988). Can comprehension be taught? A quantitative syntheses of "metacognitive" studies. *Educational Researcher, 17,* 5–8.

Harste, J. E., Woodward, V. A., & Burke, C. L. (1984). *Language stories and literacy lessons.* Portsmouth, NH: Heinemann.

Heath, S. B. (1983). *Ways with words.* New York: Cambridge University Press.

Heath, S. B., with Thomas, C. (1984). The achievement of preschool literacy for mother and child. In H. Goelman, A. Oberg, & F. Smith (Eds.), *Awakening to literacy* (pp. 51–72). Portsmouth, NH: Heinemann.

IRA. (1989). *Literacy development and prefirst grade* (Joint Statement of Concerns… prepared by the Early Childhood and Literacy Development Committee of the International Reading Association). In D. S. Strickland & L. M. Morrow (Eds.), *Emerging literacy: Young children learn to read and write.* Newark, DE: International Reading Association.

Jongsma, K. S. (1990) Intergenerational literacy: Questions and answers. *Reading Teacher, 43,* 522–523.

Karweit, N. (1989). Effective kindergarten programs and practices for students at risk. In R. E.

Slavin, N. L. Karweit, & N. A. Madden (Eds.), *Effective programs for students at risk* (pp. 103–142). Boston: Allyn & Bacon.

Kozma, R. B. (1991). Learning with media. *Review of Educational Research, 61,* 179–211.

Langer, J. A. (1986). *Children reading and writing: Structures and strategies.* Norwood, NJ: Ablex.

Levin, H. (1987). *Toward accelerated schools.* New Brunswick, NJ: Center for Policy Research in Education.

Martinez, M. G., & Roser, N. L. (1991). Children's responses to literature. In J. Flood, J. Jensen, D. Lapp, & J. R. Squire (Eds.), *The handbook of research in the teaching of the English language arts* (pp. 643–654). New York: Macmillan.

McCaleb, J. L., Borko, J., Arends, R. A., Garner, R., & Mauro, L. (1987). Innovation in teacher education: The evolution of a program. *Journal of Teacher Education, 38,* 57–64.

National Association for the Education of Young Children (NAEYC). (1985). Position statement on developmentally appropriate practice in programs for four and five year olds. *Young Children, 86,* 20–29.

Nickse, R.S. (1989, March). *The noises of literacy: An overview of intergenerational and family literacy programs.* A report (Paper No. 403J47900343) for the Office of Educational Research and Improvement, Department of Education, Washington, DC.

Olson, K., & Sulzby, E. (1991). The computer as a social/physical environment in emergent literacy. *Yearbook of the National Reading Conference, 40,* 111–118.

Palincsar, A. S. (1986). The role of dialogue in providing scaffolded instruction. *Educational Psychologist, 21*(1–2), 73–98.

Palincsar, A. S., & Brown, A. L. (1984). Reciprocal teaching of comprehension-fostering and monitoring activities. *Cognition and Instruction, 1*(1), 117–175.

Palincsar, A. S., & Brown, A. L. (1989). Classroom dialogues to promote self-regulated comprehension. In J. Brophy (Ed.), *Advances in research on teaching,* (Vol. 1, pp. 35–71). Greenwich, CT: JAI Press.

Palincsar, A. S., & Klenk, L. (1992). Fostering literacy learning in supportive contexts. *Journal of Learning Disabilities, 25*(4), 211–225, 229.

Paris, S. G., Lipson, M., & Wixson, K. (1983). Becoming a strategic reader. *Contemporary Educational Psychology, 8,* 217–227.

Pearson, P. D., & Fielding, L. (1991). *Handbook of reading research* (Vol. 2, pp. 815–860). New York: Longman.

Potts, M.W., & Popp, R.J. (1991, March). *Intergenerational literacy: Developing literacy skills of children and adults.* Paper presented at the symposium on Intergenerational literacy at Teachers College, Columbia University, New York.

Pressley, M., Johnson, C. J., Symons, S., McGoldrick, J. A., & Kurita, J. A. (1989). Strategies that improve children's memory and comprehension of text. *Elementary School Journal, 90,* 3–32.

Richardson, V., & Anders, P. L. (1991). *Reading instruction study: Final report.* Submitted to OERI, U.S. Department of Education, (Report No. G-008710014). Tucson, AZ: The University of Arizona. (ERIC ED 312359).

Richardson, V., Anders, P. L., Tidwell, D., & Lloyd, C. (1991). The relationship between teachers' beliefs and practices in reading comprehension instruction. *American Educational Research Journal, 28*(3), 559–586.

Rosenblatt, L. (1985). Viewpoints: Transaction versus interaction—A terminological rescue operation. *Research in the Teaching of English, 19,* 96–107.

Rosenblatt, L. (1991). Literacy theory. In. J. Flood, J. Jensen, D. Lapp, & J. R. Squire (Eds.), *The handbook of research in the teaching of English language arts* (pp. 57–62). New York: Macmillan.

Ruth, L. (1991). Who decides? Policymakers in English language arts education. In J. Flood, J. Jensen, D. Lapp, & J. R. Squire (Eds.), *The handbook of research in the teaching of the English language arts* (pp. 85–109). New York: Macmillan.

Slavin, R. E., Karweit, N. L., & Madden, N. A. (1989). *Effective programs for students at risk.* Needham Heights, MA: Allyn & Bacon.

Snow, C. E., Barnes, W. S., Chandler, J., Goodman, I. F., & Hemphill, J. (1991). *Unfulfilled expectations: Home and school influences on literacy.* Cambridge: Harvard University Press.

Solomon, G., Perkins, D. N., & Globerson, T. (1991). Partners in cognition: Extending human intelligence with intelligent technologies. *Educational Researcher, 20*(3), 2–9.

Spiro, R. J. (1980). Constructive processes in prose comprehension. In R. J. Spiro, B. C. Bruch, & W. F. Brewer (Eds.), *Theoretical issues in prose comprehension* (pp. 245–278). Hillsdale, NJ: Lawrence Erlbaum Associates.

Stein, N. L., & Glenn, C. G. (1979). An analysis of story comprehension in elementary school children. In R. O. Freedle (Ed.), *New directions in discourse comprehension* (Vol. 2, pp. 53–120). Norwood, NJ: Ablex.

Sulzby, E. (1983, September). *Beginning readers' developing knowledges about written language* (Final report to the National Institute of Education [NIE-G-80-0176]). Evanston, IL: Northwestern University.

Sulzby, E. (1985). Children's emergent reading of favorite storybooks: A developmental study. *Reading Research Quarterly, 20*(4), 458–481.

Sulzby, E. (1989). Assessment of writing and of children's language while writing. In L. Morrow & J. Smith (Eds.), *The role of assessment and measurement in early literacy instruction* (pp. 83–109). Englewood Cliffs, NJ: Prentice-Hall.

Sulzby, E., & Teale, W. H. (1987, November). *Young children's storybook reading: Longitudinal study of parent–child interaction and children's independent functioning* (Final report to the Spencer Foundation). Ann Arbor, MI: University of Michigan.

Sulzby, E., & Teale, W. H. (1991) Emergent literacy. In R. Barr, M. L. Kamil, P. Mosenthal, & P. D. Pearson (Eds.), *Handbook of reading research* (Vol. 2, pp. 727–757). New York: Longman.

Taylor, D., & Dorsey-Gaines, C. (1988). *Growing up literate: Learning from innercity families.* Portsmouth, NH: Heinemann.

Teale, W. H. (1986). Home background and young children's literacy development. In W. H. Teale & E. Sulzby (Eds.), *Emergent literacy: Writing and reading* (pp. 173–206). Norwood, NJ: Ablex.

Teale, W. H., & Sulzby, E. (1986). Emergent literacy as a perspective for examining how children become writers and readers. In W. H. Teale & E. Sulzby (Eds.), *Emergent literacy: Writing and Reading* (pp. vii–xxv). Norwood, NJ: Ablex.

Themed issue on Redirecting Assessment. (1989, April). *Educational Leadership, 46*(7).

Tierney, R. J. (1991). Studies of reading and writing growth: Longitudinal research on literacy development. In J. Flood, J. Jensen, D. Lapp, & J. R. Squire (Eds.), *The handbook of research in the teaching of the English language arts* (pp. 176–194). New York: Macmillan.

Tierney, R. J., & Cunningham, J. W. (1984). Research on teaching comprehension. In P. D. Pearson, R. Barr, M. L. Kamil, & P. Mosenthal (Eds.), *Handbook of reading research* (Vol. I, pp. 609–655). New York: Longman.

Tierney, R. J., & Pearson, P. D. (1983). Toward a composing model of reading. *Language Arts, 60,* 568–580.

Vygotsky, L. S. (1978). *Mind in society: The development of higher psychological processes.* (M. Cole, V. John-Steiner, S. Scribner, & E. Souberman, Eds.). Cambridge, MA: Harvard University Press.

Vygotsky, L. S. (1981). The genesis of higher mental functions. In J. V. Wertsch (Ed.), *The concept of activity in Soviet psychology* (pp. 144–188). Armonk, NY: M. E. Sharpe.

Waller, R. (1991). Typography and discourse. In R. Barr, M. L. Kamil, & P. Mosenthal, & P. D. Pearson (Eds.), *Handbook of reading research* (Vol. 2, pp. 341–380). New York: Longman.

Wildman, T. M., & Niles, J.A. (1987). Reflective teachers: Tensions between abstractions and realities. *Journal of Teacher Education, 38,* 25–31.

Wood, F., McQuarrie, F., Thompson, S. F. (1982). Practitioners and professors agree on effective staff development practices. *Educational Leadership, 39,* 28–31.

4

On Reading: A Survey of Recent Research and Proposals for the Future

Isabel L. Beck
University of Pittsburgh

It is often difficult to decide how to limit a discussion of an enormous domain, and the state of the art of reading research and practice is, indeed, an enormous domain. Two general ways of constraining a domain are to briefly touch on many of its topics, or to examine a limited, smaller number of topics. The latter is always my preference. As such, I chose to limit this discussion to issues about the reader and the text. As a result, numerous important topics and issues (e.g., assessment, motivation, the reading/writing connection) that interact with the reader and what she or he reads will not be considered. Their exclusion is not meant to imply that they lack importance.

This chapter starts with a discussion of two theoretical orientations (cognitive and social) that have influenced both theory and practice. A section on the reader follows, with a discussion of research on comprehension in which the two theoretical orientations emerge. The discussion concludes with perspectives on setting a research agenda. The next section, on texts, has a parallel structure; it reviews recent developments in research on the nature of texts and concludes with some observations about future research. The third section focuses on a set of topics that are related to instruction in beginning reading and offers consideration of key concerns that research in that area now confronts. The final section summarizes recommendations for the research agenda.

THEORETICAL ORIENTATIONS

The state-of-the-art in reading research, since the 1970s, has been profoundly influenced by the scientific inquiry on human cognition that took shape in the late 1950s and 1960s (e.g., Bruner, 1957; Miller, 1965), that is, by what has come to be known as the "cognitive revolution" (Gardner, 1985). More recently, theories about the social nature of learning (Vygotsky, 1978) and examinations of the social contexts in which learning occurs (Resnick, 1989) and the social organization of classrooms (Weinstein, 1991) have begun playing a strong role in both reading research and practice.

Reading as an Individual Cognitive Activity

The cognitive orientation to reading, with its new forms of theorizing and new research paradigms, addressed the complexity of the reading process by attempting to understand the mental processes involved in reading, that is, what the reader does while reading. Earlier, the emphasis was on the products of reading, that is, what the reader remembered after reading. In the current cognitive view, reading consists of a complex set of coordinated mental processes that includes perceptual, linguistic, and conceptual operations. The mechanics of these operations range from encoding the letters that appear on the printed page, to determining the referent of a particular phrase or word, to following the structure of the text, such as a story or exposition. In the course of reading, readers build a representation of the concepts and events that are being described, a representation that draws heavily on what they already know about the topic. To comprehend a text, readers must perform all these mental operations, many of them concurrently.

The present view of reading, then, is that it is an interactive process in which the reader constructs meaning by integrating text information with information already in memory. The interactive conception contrasts with earlier views that reading proceeded in sequential steps, in either a bottom-up or top-down process. According to the bottom-up view, the reader relies on the text to get to the ideas; that is, he or she proceeds from identifying words, to putting them together into meaningful clauses and sentences, to establishing the meaning of the text. In the top-down view, the reader's ideas about the topic of a text allow an initial interpretation of the information on the page, and confirmation or rejection of that interpretation comes as he or she samples the print.

The interactive view generated by more than two decades of cognitive analyses assumes that the information the reader supplies and the information on the page influence each other simultaneously to produce comprehension (Just & Carpenter, 1987; Perfetti, 1985; Rumelhart, 1977; Stanovich, 1980). As the reader perceives visual information from the text, she or he calls on a number of sources of knowledge. These include awareness of letter–sound correspondences and spelling patterns, knowledge of word meaning, knowledge of syntactic possibilities and language patterns, and memory of the preceding text. The sources interact to help the reader compile information about the textual input, attribute meaning to it, and integrate it with what has come before. Thus, the reader is able to construct the larger meaning of the text.

A key theme that emerged from these cognitive analyses of the mental processes entailed in reading is that the reader's extant knowledge has a pervasive influence on comprehension. Attempts to develop more precise theories of how knowledge is represented, accessed, and used during reading now lie at the heart of this work. Related attempts to delineate the characteristics of the structure of texts, as they influence comprehension, have become important to reading research. The influence on comprehension of a number of textual characteristics was identified experimentally, and this work testifies to the value of cognitive analyses of reading.

Taken together, much progress has been made in understanding the nature of the reading process and the nature of the text's influences on comprehension. The most fundamental change of the past decades is that reading is no longer viewed either as a matter of extracting meaning from the printed page or using the text to confirm or reject an initial interpretation; rather, reading is now seen as a complex cognitive process in which readers actively construct meaning on the basis of information in a text and information in memory.

Reading and the Social Context of Learning

Recently, cognitive analyses of reading have been broadened to consider the ways in which social contexts, particularly in the classroom, influence reading comprehension and one's capacity to learn from texts. If cognitive research has allowed us to "look into the mind," that is, to make inferences about the way the mind receives, stores, and accesses information, then interest in the social context extends our attention to the influence of the environment on these processes. This orientation does not conflict with cognitive approaches, rather it enlarges the focus to social dimensions of cognition.

The development of skills in reading and the acquisition of higher levels of literacy occur in social settings, be they classroom/school environments, the home, or the workplace. In the early 1970s, scholars from several domains, most notably cognitive scientists and anthropologists, began "to study forms of social participation that have positive effects on reasoning and that redistribute knowledge through a group involved in collaboration" (Heath, 1991). Researchers examined the social and linguistic nature of these various contexts, and looked across contexts as well. (For example, see Barr, 1989, for the impact of ability grouping on the social organization of literacy instruction; Bloome & Green, 1984, for a sociolinguistic orientation; Cazden, 1986, for a discussion of classroom discourse; Heath, 1991, for a cultural-historical orientation; Hoffman, 1991, for teacher and school effects in learning to read.)

The development of literacy before formal schooling and the influence of out-of-school contexts during schooling notwithstanding, the classroom is, for many, the primary setting in which literacy is acquired. But some researchers observed that "the classroom is not a homogenized glob" (Kounin & Sherman, cited in Weinstein, 1991, p. 150). Indeed, classrooms are complex social environments that elicit varying social behaviors from both teachers and pupils. Students' attention and participation, for example, are influenced by external events, as shaped by the teacher, and the extent to which students work interdependently has major effects on their attention and participation (Gump, cited in Weinstein, 1991).

The interdependence of participants in learning activities is an important theme in recent educational research. Researchers who studied learning in real-life situations point to critical features that distinguish it from learning in school. Resnick (1987), among others, suggested that the interdependence so evident in real-life activities needs to be implemented in the classroom: "Socially shared intellectual work that (is) organized around joint accomplishment of tasks" (p. 18) better supports effective learning than does individual work in classroom exercises. Classroom practices have been criticized specifically for decontextualizing knowledge and skills, stripping them of the cultural and physical supports of the disciplinary practices in which they are actually used (Brown, Collins, & Duguid, 1989). Thus, the calls for "situated learning" and "authentic" texts and tests have become frequent. (The importance now accorded the social context in learning will emerge through the descriptions of recent trends in reading research.)

THE READER

Current understandings of the processes involved when the reader engages with a text were derived from research about the nature of normal skilled reading. These understandings, which are deep and complex, have, for the most part, been developed from fine-grained analyses and research. As would be expected, the level and form of the resultant knowledge were not articulated to make direct connections with educational practice. The theories, however, encouraged educationally oriented researchers to focus attention on whether and how mental processes involved in comprehension (those that had been thought of as unfolding in "the black box") might be influenced. And, as such, instructional studies aimed at improving comprehension of both narrative and expository text have proliferated and yielded valuable results (see Pearson & Fielding, 1991, for an excellent review of these studies).

Research on Comprehension

Although attempts to improve students' comprehension are far from new, the recent generation of instructional studies of comprehension are qualitatively different from those of the past. The major themes of these studies map back to the interactive, constructive view of skilled reading. For instance, what the reader knows about the topic of the material to be read is a critical determinant of comprehension, and investigators in numerous studies designed interventions to build or activate students' background knowledge about the topics in a selection. Furthermore, because differences in the structure of text genres (e.g., narratives and expository texts are organized differently) affect comprehension, some studies focused on fostering students' understanding of these structures. Teaching students about text structure has been particularly prevalent with expository texts because exposition, unlike narrative, does not follow a predictable pattern in delivering information and therefore presents special difficulty.

A striking difference between these studies and earlier instructional research can be attributed to the cognitive orientation. In earlier work, students were told or induced to employ a certain technique; little, if anything, was communicated about how or why the technique might be helpful. In the newer work, students are made aware of how and where the technique might be valuable. As such, the emphasis is on putting students in touch with their own thought processes.

In light of the understanding that readers construct meaning by relating background knowledge to text information, by integrating text information from different places in a selection, and by identifying and focusing on important information; researchers developed and studied strategies for encouraging such processing. Work in this area falls under several rubrics: comprehension monitoring, metacognitive instruction, techniques of self-monitoring or self-regulation. No matter the label, the general notion is that thorough comprehension requires readers' active engagement in constructing meaning. Getting students to engage with texts and develop interpretations requires helping them to monitor their cognitive processes, to gauge the extent to which they comprehend incoming information and perceive areas of difficulty, as well as to initiate strategies to repair the problems. In essence, young readers must be helped to strive for the kind of active comprehension that is characteristic of mature readers.

Beginning in the early 1980s, questions about the cultivation of comprehension-monitoring skills led to consideration of social influences on learning. One trend involved studying students of varied ability working together to achieve an academic goal. There is a large literature in which this cooperative learning orientation was described. Although cooperative learning is not limited to reading, evaluations of its effectiveness were conducted with reading and reading-related tasks (Johnson et al., 1981; Slavin, 1989).

Questions remain, however, about the extent to which various social contexts support and engender the development of generative text-processing strategies and higher levels of thinking about text. The kind of cognitive interactions that cooperative learning produces and their impact on individual performances were not sufficiently analyzed (Bossert, 1988-1989). "In depth consideration of the actual thinking processes affected by such settings is rare" (Brown & Palincsar, 1989, p. 397) and the mechanisms by which they are improved have yet to be described fully. Although the literature suggests that cooperative settings produce better learning out-comes than do individual activities, the better outcomes may not extend beyond literal learning of the content, to such processes as "elaboration of ideas, analysis and problem solving" (Sharan, 1980, p. 255). Thus, there are calls for accounts of how specific social interactions mediate "higher liter-acy"—for our purposes here, the thinking involved in the constructive nature of comprehension. That is, there is a need to conduct fine-grained analyses, to go beyond identifying the conditions under which learning is improved.

Such work has been initiated. It focused on considerations of the quality of classroom discussions in terms of the cognitive processes that certain participatory structures engender. (See, e.g., Au & Kawakami, 1984; Brown & Palincsar, 1989; O'Flahavan, 1989). This work represents an intersection be-tween cognitive and social perspectives that promises significant advances.

Perspectives on Future Research on Reading Comprehension

There is evidence that instructional research on comprehension has found its way into the practicing community. Education journals and programs for state and national meetings that practitioners attend are full of new language: The role of background knowledge, the interactive nature of reading, metacognition, strategic reading, and the like have become com-mon parlance. In this section, I probe the depth of practitioners' under-standings of reading research and offer a suggestion about reading research that may serve to deepen what practitioners learn from research, as well as raise the quality of the research.

Traditional tactics for articulating the implications of research on reading and other forms of learning to teachers include crafting articles for practi-tioner-oriented journals and giving presentations and workshops. Synoptic publications such as *What Works* and fuller policy documents such as *Becoming a Nation of Readers* offer generalizations about framing practices that are grounded in research. The limitation of generalizations, however, as William James observed 100 years ago, is that "no one sees further into a generalization than his knowledge of the details allows."

Exposing the Details.   The accuracy of James' assertion was brought home to me by one response to an instructional study that my colleagues and I published in the *Reading Research Quarterly* (Beck, Omanson, & McKeown, 1982). In this article, we reported that upgrading background information and asking a set of coherent questions produced better comprehension of several stories in a basal reader than did the use of the commercial version's background information and questions.

Some time after the article appeared, an experienced practitioner telephoned us to say quite directly that she didn't like the study: "I don't understand what you did," she explained. It appeared that she was put off by the technical terms, statistics, and so forth, so we sent her another version of the study that we had subsequently written for a different outlet. Another telephone call came, in which she indicated that we had missed the point of her first call: It was not that she had not understood the first article; it was that she did not understand what we "really did." The second manuscript had only provided, in nontechnical language, the same results that we had presented in the original article.

Eventually, my colleagues and I realized that the caller was dissatisfied with the discursive descriptions of the conditions in the study, so we sent her the stimulus materials: the sets of questions and the experimenter's script for each condition. The scripts were very precise, because the conditions had been presented to individuals, and contained branches to handle idiosyncratic responses. This tenacious critic's response to the stimulus materials was unambiguous: This was the "stuff" that we should have published in the first place.

The research term for stuff is *instrumentation*. The instrumentation, which includes materials, procedures, and methodology that educational researchers develop for such instructional studies, takes various forms. Some instruments are very closely designed; for instance, scripted directions and/or explanations for the experimenter/teacher, a text that treats a specific topic, several text versions about the same topic, sets of questions that were framed to assess comprehension of a specific theme, and graphic organizers. Many of the newer instructional studies do not involve the implementation of such items, rather they involve researchers collaborating with teachers in changing the teacher's role and the structure and character of the instructional discourse. The focus of these studies is to examine the outcomes when teachers encourage their students to engage, say, in an active search for meaning. The teacher explains and models techniques for monitoring comprehension processes and has the students practice the techniques. Such *self-monitoring* techniques, which can be seen as *comprehension-fostering strategies* (Pearson & Fielding, 1991), focused on questioning, summarizing, and predicting (see Palincsar & Brown, 1984; Paris, Cross, & Lipson, 1984).

Dissemination of detailed information about instrumentation is valuable for several reasons—ones that accord well with James' observation about the relative utility of generalizations. First, the instrumentation that is used in any study, be it more basic psychological work or an instructional intervention, needs to be emphasized because *it* represents the underlying theory. The instrumentation embodies, translates, and implements conceptions of learning and performance that drive the work. Implied here is the concern that the translation of theory into instructional studies may not be getting the attention it needs. Toward that end, the instrumentation in these studies needs to be opened to careful public scrutiny.

What constitutes public scrutiny of closely designed instrumentation like scripts or question sets is straightforward. Public scrutiny for the more generic techniques, techniques in which the teacher implements models or changes in instructional engagements, require that actual transcripts, across time, of what the teacher and students did and said be made available. For these kinds of interventions, Palincsar and Brown's (1984) reports of the research on reciprocal teaching are an excellent model because their descriptions include extensive transcripts of actual implementations of the procedures.

Presently, most reports of instructional research published in journals offer generalizations about effective practices and only discursive descriptions of the instrumentation. Sometimes an example is provided in an appendix. Given that theories are abstractions, one cannot understand the extent to which a theory worked in practice, or was weakened, or failed to work, unless one can scrutinize the stuff that implemented the theory. Thus, scrutiny of the instrumentation can be a major encouragement—or discouragement—to the adoption of new practices in education.

As it now stands, although supplying information about instrumentation may be among the best ways to articulate knowledge that can influence educational practice, that information very seldom finds its way into the archival system or practitioners' hands. That the tenacious caller was not satisfied until she saw the examples was not an unusual incident. When practitioners encounter educational research, usually in specifically targeted journals and edited volumes, they tend to find it "interesting," but where they can, they latch on to examples, that is, to "stuff." They need knowledge of the details in order to see into the generalizations. Expansion of the archival system to include such materials could be of great advantage to both researchers and practitioners. Moreover, publishers are important players in the educational arena, and they would benefit from requiring researchers to craft their interventions—be they strategies, the design of social contexts, the development of more coherent texts—in ways that would help others see beneath the labels. Thus, the argument is that detailed materials and procedures—that is, examples, demonstrators, transcripts of instructional engagements—are required to make generalizations meaningful.

Engineering Instructional Research.   The value of Palincsar and Brown's work with reciprocal teaching goes beyond their clarifying underlying theory and principles by exposing the details of the research; they "engineered" reciprocal teaching at every phase of implementation. They tested it against quality control conditions, separated the features and tested them independently, moved it to larger environments, explored it with different subject matters, examined its uses in other hands, and more (Brown & Palincsar, 1982, 1989). This kind of sustained engineering is costly, but it should be encouraged and supported.

Essential to the success of such engineering is that it be done by those who have command of the intricacies of the theories and the many interactions involved in innovations in education, that is by researchers who work in collaboration with practitioners who understand the complexities of classroom/school environments. Nearly a decade of evaluation and refinement has passed since the very first reciprocal teaching study was published (Brown & Palincsar, 1982). Long-term crafting and engineering of theoretically based instructional interventions should become customary in reading research. Detailed demonstrations, like reports of instrumentation, are the linchpins to understanding the generalizations spawned by fundamental analyses of the reading process. The details may well fade in memory, but the generalizations may become lasting and flexible, if they are rooted.

TEXTS

By definition, reading involves interactions with written language (texts); consequently, reading researchers have long been concerned with the nature of texts. Before cognitive analyses were available, characterizations of texts centered on readability formulas that predicted text difficulty by considering sentence length and vocabulary complexity. However, it was theoretically established and widely accepted for more than a decade that these two variables do not influence comprehension (Kintsch & Vipond, 1979).

Research on Text

Recent work went beyond the examination of discrete surface features of text. Investigators were able to describe text features that influence comprehension directly by taking into account the structure of texts (i.e., how texts are organized) and how readers represent incoming information in memory. Recent models of text structure describe how readers process the material; they incorporate notions of the interaction between extant knowledge and new information and describe that interaction's effects on the reader's representation.

Formal efforts to create models of text structure reflect the concern with issues of representation. One thrust is the development of story grammars, which are schematic representations of narratives that readers presumably use in comprehending and recalling stories (Mandler & Johnson, 1977; Rumelhart, 1975; Stein & Glenn, 1979).

Another thrust is the articulation of schemes for representing the relations among small units of text, including nonnarratives, which are assumed to characterize the conception of content that builds as the individual reads. In this way, every concept in the text, rather than general categories of text content—as in story grammars—is considered. Because these models are based on smaller units or microlevel representations, they differ from story grammars and are applicable to expositions (Frederiksen, 1975; Kintsch, 1974; Meyer, 1975).

Although the formal models were developed mainly for cognitive analyses of reading, understandings of text variables that influence comprehension that the formal models yielded were useful to educational reading researchers in evaluating and revising texts. These researchers determined criteria for well-structured texts of various types and showed that many current textbooks fail to meet these criteria. Anderson and Armbruster (1984) created the concept of *considerateness* as a goal in text design. Beck, McKeown, Omanson, and Pople (1984) studied issues of text coherence on the basis of formal models (e.g., Trabasso, Secco, & van den Broek, 1984) and revised texts and assessed the effect of increased *coherence* on children's comprehension (see also Beck, McKeown, Sinatra, & Loxterman, 1991).

Concern about the inadequacies of the materials students read in their school books is now deeper than ever. Frequently, complaints are voiced about the "dumbing down" of text materials, an outcome attributed to the widespread use of readability formulas. Documentation of the negative effects of adapting trade book materials to formulas (Anderson & Davison, 1988) may have fueled the larger community's concern about the quality of the materials that students read in their school books. But school books, especially at the elementary level, are not independent objects; they are one component of large instructional systems. In reading, they are part of basal reading programs and in the content areas, they are part of textbook series.

Instructional Systems: Basal Reading Programs and Textbook Series

In the late 1970s and on into the 1980s, there was an explosion of descriptive analyses of basal reading programs and content area textbooks. (References to many of these studies can be found in Chall & Squire, 1991.) In addition to issues about the quality of the texts in the commercially available programs, researchers scrutinized the instructional recommendations the teachers' editions provide for everything from teaching phonics to developing vocabulary and background knowledge, from questions for discussion and follow-up activities to students' workbooks and tests, and more. And, to lesser or greater degrees, they found the commercial materials of the late 1970s and on into the mid-1980s wanting on all such dimensions.

However, even in the current climate of reform, where there are calls for throwing out traditional school books, like it or not, many schools will continue to use commercially available materials. Thus, we have a responsibility to encourage their improvement. Moreover, there is a relationship between curricular materials and teacher education that suggests that the benefits of improving the textbook programs would be twofold.

In a longitudinal study in which students in two preservice teacher preparation programs were tracked, Ball and Feiman-Nemser (1988) found that "all of them developed the impression that if they wanted to be good teachers they should avoid following textbooks and relying on teachers' guides" (p. 401). For these trainees, however, the student teaching usually involved adhering to textbooks and guides. As a result, many were unprepared to handle the materials that they had to use. Even more importantly, when they attempted to depart from the prepared texts and create their own lessons, they stumbled and failed to capture the essence of the teaching point. Forced to adapt, some were eventually able to use the teachers' guide as scaffolding to better understand and teach the topic. Ball and Feiman-Nemser argue that teacher educators need to "teach beginning elementary teachers how to learn from using published curricular materials" (p. 401). Those who had used the presumably poor materials seemed to learn from them, but how much better would their learning have been if they had had good materials and good models?

Are better models, those based on findings from recent research, appearing in the newer school materials? The instructional suggestions and recommendations for learning activities in the newer materials, those with late 1980s and early 1990s copyrights, indicate that the programs incorporated the newer terminology (e.g., metacognition, constructing meaning, the reading-writing connection). But, how those labels are realized in the materials for teachers and activities for children cannot be determined without thorough scrutiny, and the latest versions are too new for that to have happened.

Perspectives on Future Research on School Books

It is important that, in the next period of reading research, researchers continue the practice of analyzing instructional materials and making their findings public. This continued scrutiny will serve two purposes. It will inform the public about the quality of the materials that are available, and, even more importantly, it will serve to raise the quality of materials by pointing out where they implemented a notion well, where they weakened a potential impact, what they should not have implemented, and what they should have included but did not.

CRITICAL CONCERNS IN BEGINNING READING AND INSTRUCTION

The key issues of reading as a cognitive process discussed to this point are certainly relevant to beginning reading. That is, the beginning reader must engage in construction of meaning and interact with texts, the character of which is of importance to that process. In beginning reading, however, there is an additional major and controversial issue, that is, the role of ortho- graphic knowledge. In practical terms, this issue raises questions of whether, when, how much, and what kind of phonics should be used to support word recognition.

Approaches to Early Reading

Theoretical concerns about the extent to which a child's facility in reading is fostered by increasing knowledge of language and the world or, alterna- tively, by the development of orthographic knowledge and the use of orthographic information (i.e., the development of word recognition knowledge and skills) play a part in most discussions of beginning reading. The first position is taken by Goodman (1976), who suggested that ortho- graphic information is not critical. "Skill in reading involves not greater precision, but more accurate first guesses, based on better sampling tech- niques, greater control over language structure, broadened experiences and increased conceptual development" (p. 504). The second position is repre- sented by Ehri (1978), who sees "word recognition as the major hurdle faced by the beginner" (p. 1).

Debates about these theoretical differences and their implications for beginning reading instruction (i.e., the degree of emphasis that should be placed on the child's discovering knowledge of orthography through com- munication-focused instruction, and systematically directing the child's attention to the orthography) have been around for decades. The merits of these differing approaches were once argued about under such labels as *whole word* versus *phonics*, or *meaning emphasis* versus *code emphasis*. As we moved into the 1990s, this controversy became, in part, related to philo- sophical, social, and political issues that continue to exert great influence, all of which are represented in the whole-language movement. It is worth- while, here, to raise some of the key questions in early reading that are associated with the continuum of theoretical differences.

Whole Language.   When a perfect expression exists of one's view of a particular matter, it makes sense to use it. Pearson's (1989) characterization of the whole-language movement already put my own thoughts to paper:

> The reading field seems to have a special knack for attracting wide-scale reforms—one after another, after another, after another. But never have I witnessed anything like the rapid spread of the whole-language movement. Pick your metaphor—an epidemic, wildfire, manna from heaven—whole language has spread so rapidly throughout North America that it is a fact of life in literacy curriculum and research. (p. 231)

The whole-language movement is, for many of its proponents, not simply about reading and related literacy, but an "educational paradigm" that involves concerns about "fundamental questions such as: What is reality? Where do facts come from? What is truth? How should power be distributed?" (Edelsky, 1990, p. 7). Watson captured the enormity of the phenomenon in the introduction to her article, "Defining and Describing Whole Language," by suggesting that "whole language is a spirit, a philosophy, a movement" (1989, pp. 129-130). Thus, it is impossible to do justice to the whole-language movement in this short space, both because of the many dimensions involved and because it has been suggested that only those who are members of the whole-language community can discuss it adequately (Edelsky, 1990). (See the November, 1989 special edition on whole language of the *Elementary School Journal* for a collection of articles by some of the leaders in the movement.) But the research issues that pertain to whole language merit attention and are discussed in a later section.

The following discussion turns to emergent literacy, a recent phenomenon that is related to whole language and is revealing of issues in the debates about beginning reading in that its theoretical underpinnings tilt toward a more naturalistic orientation to literacy development. In terms of reading, the notion is that the acquisition of reading tends to emerge from oral language development and growth in knowledge of the world.

Emergent Literacy. The term *emergent literacy* was coined by Marie Clay (1966), and adopted by educational investigators in the 1980s to describe "the reading and writing behaviors that precede and develop into conventional literacy." The orientation is that "young children—even 1- and 2-year-olds—are in the process of becoming literate." Although this literacy is not manifested in conventional ways, it is viewed as "understandings or hypotheses about literacy" (p. 728).

Emergent literacy researchers have studied emergent storybook reading and writing through naturalistic, particularly ethnographic, techniques. They have produced rich descriptions of storybook reading as a "socially created, interactive activity (whose patterns) change over time with children's increasing age, knowledge, and experience." They have also identified "variations in storybook-reading patterns of interaction (that) affect children's development differentially" (Sulzby & Teale, 1991, p. 731). This literature provides insights about what children learn from storybook reading that facilitates conventional literacy.

Research on emergent writing has not gone as far as emergent reading research. However, observations of children who write before they learn to read, by inventing their own spellings, are relevant. A child who engages in invented spelling is showing evidence that she or he has some sense of the alphabetic principle, which holds that meaning-bearing units of language (words) are composed of nonmeaning-bearing units (letters), and that these letters become attached to units of speech rather than units of meaning.

Phonemic Awareness.   *Phonemic awareness* is a relatively new term for an individual's understanding that spoken words are comprised of speech sounds that are smaller than syllables, that is, of phonemes. Much of the recent work on phonemic awareness was done by educational psychologists interested in examining its relationship to reading ability. There are, however, major questions concerning the direction of that relationship: Is phonemic awareness required for early reading, does it result from learning to read, or does it develop in a reciprocal relationship with reading? (See, for example, the July 1987 *Merrill-Palmer Quarterly: Journal of Developmental Psychology*, an invitational issue on Children's Reading and the Development of Phonological Awareness, and more recent discussions in Ehri, 1991; Juel, 1991; Stanovich, 1991; Sulzby & Teale, 1991.) Although questions about the direction of the relationship have not been completely resolved, there seems to be ample evidence that some degree of phonemic awareness is important for learning to read and that good phonemic awareness is a powerful facilitator of word recognition.

Phonics.   *Phonics* is an umbrella term for instructional strategies for teaching spelling–sound correspondences as a means of developing young readers' ability to recognize words. Research on word recognition has a long history in reading research. Until about the 1970s, it may have been the most active area of work. Over the last 20 years, although most reading researchers turned their attention to comprehension, a smaller number produced a steady stream of psychologically rigorous word recognition research (Ehri, 1991; Stanovich, 1991). Adams' (1990) recent book reviewed this literature, making it more accessible to a broad audience. In addition, over the 1980s, studies that looked at the effects of phonics instruction have continued to confirm that "on the average, children who are taught phonics get off to a better start in learning to read than children who are not taught phonics" (Anderson, Hiebert, Scott, & Wilkinson, 1985, p. 50). Yet the appearance of this conclusion in the widely distributed *Becoming a Nation of Readers* may, in part, explain the renewed intensity of the debate.

Perspectives on Future Research on Beginning Reading

The most basic issue in the constellation that now surrounds early reading is the development of models of the acquisition of reading. But this is a complicated business, much more complicated than the development of models of competent skilled reading.

Comprehensive Models of the Acquisition of Reading.   Any attempt to track the acquisition of reading must confront the huge individual differences in young children's reading-related knowledge, experience, and motivation/interest. These differences are due partly to factors inherent in a child and partly to environmental factors as they interact with the child. Add to these individual differences variations that children encounter in reading instruction (e.g., phonics, writing, work sheets, authentic literacy), as well as differences in the social structure and climate of their classrooms and schools.

The fundamental question, of course, is *whether each of these issues matters in the acquisition of reading*. The reading research community sees all of them as having a potentially significant influence on the acquisition of reading and related literacy, as a quick look at the pages of the 1991 *Handbook of Reading Research* shows. Of course, there is nothing new about the view that the child herself, her larger social community, and the specifics of the instruction she receives influence learning. What may be new is researchers asking, across theoretical orientations, for broader, more comprehensive views of the acquisition of literacy. Following are a sprinkling of these views:

> Research on (both reading ability and disability) must deal with the factors that are known to influence reading as valuable sources of information.... Factors both internal and external to the reader (must be taken into account). (Wixson & Lipson, 1991, p. 561)

> Virtually all of the research available has failed to evaluate or adequately control for the environmental and/or educational deficits that may cause a reading disorder. (Vellutino & Denckla, 1991, p. 602)

We lack a comprehensive model of reading acquisition, one that would incorporate the various psychological, social, and instructional components that contribute to the process of learning to read. (Juel, 1991, p. 759)

Clearly, we need to consider a range of factors, and we need to consider them over time. The question, then, becomes how to achieve that goal most effectively.

Multiperspective Studies. The approach I would suggest is related to issues that Mosenthal raised in an as yet unpublished paper that Wixson and Lipson (1991) discussed. (I may well be taking Mosenthal's notions out of context. If that is the case, I apologize.) I was impressed by these characterizations:

> Reading researchers have operated in the past as a largely divided community. The result has been a proliferation of independent and sometimes competing solutions. In independently pursuing these problems, reading researchers have tended to place the integrity of their specific research community above that of the reading-research community as a whole. Progress will require reading researchers to see themselves as members of a common community with a common goal. (Wixson & Lipson, 1991, p. 565)

Given the state of our knowledge, multiperspective studies that track children's acquisition of reading and writing from when they are about ages 3 or 4 until they are 7- or 8-year-olds are clearly needed. One absolutely critical requirement in this endeavor would be establishing teams in which there are at least two principal investigators who represent diverging theoretical orientations (e.g., a more psychological orientation and a more naturalistic orientation). It is simply a fact of life that differences in philosophical and theoretical orientations pervade not only research, but also most human endeavors—and not only in the social sciences and humanities, but also in the other sciences, as well. Researchers' theoretical perspectives significantly influence their choices of focus of study, their methods and the measures that they employ, and the rules of evidence that they use to draw inferences from their data. Hence, we will never move toward more comprehensive models if multiperspective studies are not designed from the get go.

Multiperspective studies could be mounted with an investigator from a particular orientation securing consulting help from researchers from a different orientation. I am not sanguine about that approach. The debates about beginning reading are too longstanding and have taken on a life of their own. The suggestion here is for the strongest implementation, for multiperspective studies by principal investigators with deep commitments to differing orientations. The aim would not be a consensus or an averaging of views, but the inclusion of their orientations. Most importantly, this inclusion should be integral to every phase of the design and implementation of the research.

The problems and obstacles notwithstanding (sociological, epistemological, and logistical), with strong support (appropriate funding for an extended time period) this may be the time to mount the effort. The calls to do so across theoretical boundaries exist, and the approval and interest of the reading research community might be forthcoming. Unless we directly confront the issues involved in the development of comprehensive models of the acquisition of reading, comprehensive models of the acquisition of reading will remain confined to the "Looks to the Future" sections of researchers' papers.

Pursuing Phonemic Awareness.   As noted, there is evidence that young children can be taught to uncover and manipulate the phonological elements in words and that such experiences enhance early reading acquisition (Lundberg, Frost, & Peterson, 1988). The evidence, however, does not extend to important issues in designing effective phonemic training. Should written letters and words be used? When might it be developmentally most appropriate to introduce children to various games or tasks? Which individual differences need to be taken into account in decisions about the timing and nature of training for phonemic awareness? Work in this area should be pursued, particularly in training studies by those who have control of the core issues and who understand how to interest young children.

Pursuing the Role of Early Writing in Learning to Read. Observations that some children, particularly those from language-rich environments, attempt to write words and more extended ideas by "inventing" spelling, even before they can read, have generated the term *emergent writing*. One important next step in research on emergent writing would be to examine closely the role of this spontaneous emergent writing in learning to read. An additional step should be taken as well: Research should be launched to assess the benefits of encouraging early writing, in both its invented and conventional forms.

As research along these lines proceeds, distinctions should be made between emergent writing, encouraging invented spelling, and encouraging conventional writing. Encouraging invented spelling is different from emergent writing in that it does not assume that such invention will occur spontaneously. Rather, because some young children do spontaneously attempt to write, some teachers and parents are encouraging their children to write their ideas using their own unique ways to do so. No emergence is taken for granted.

Encouraging conventional writing is related to encouraging invented spelling, but it involves helping the child to see how his rendition is related to conventional writing, or showing him how it might be written conventionally. The *Reading Recovery Program* (Pinnell, 1989) takes this latter tactic. In each session, "the teacher helps the child construct the message in several ways—prompting independent trials, writing for the child, or helping the child to make a sound analysis of words" (p. 168). Although evaluation studies of Reading Recovery do not allow us to assess the contributions of separate activities, there is reason to consider the composing and writing component a significant feature of the program's success. Reading Recovery's encouragement of writing may be an excellent phonics technique in that it supports attention to the orthography. Thus, research on the role of composing and writing in the acquisition of reading should be pursued.

Evaluating and Understanding the Influence of Whole Language on Children's Literacy Achievement. Given the widespread attention to the whole-language movement, the field needs to come to understand the influence of this approach on children's acquisition of reading and reading related knowledge and skills. But there are problems to be confronted here, both methodological and political. One methodological problem is the enormous variations across implementations of the whole-language approach. Consider the following description of a first-grade classroom.

The environment was designed around a number of learning centers, which were supported by community volunteers. These centers provided:

opportunities for children to dictate stories to an adult (teacher or community volunteer); a place where directed, presequenced spelling–sound instruction occurred; a library corner with many excellent trade books; a typical small group reading circle in which a basal preprimer and all its apparatuses were used; a writing corner in which things needed for writing were available; and various other facilities.

This classroom had an array of characteristics: it might be seen as an *open classroom*, as *activity-centered instruction*, and as *adaptive education* as well. After observing the classroom, however, a visiting principal said something like: "Now I understand what whole language is." But what went on in that classroom did not accord with *my* notion of whole language. A basal preprimer was consistently used; phonics was imposed—not derived from authentic literacy activities. These tactics would not be acceptable to the purists. Features that were consistent with a whole-language approach included the teacher's often playing the role of facilitator, the extensive engagement with trade books, the many opportunities for the children to write, and the encouragement of peer-peer interactions. These features, however, are found in many classroom environments that do not consider themselves whole language.

Thus, any attempt to come to understand the effectiveness of something as global as whole language collides with the familiar problem that many things are called things that they are not, and many things are not called what they are. This problem was realized during the 1960s in the Cooperative Reading Projects that the U.S. Office of Education sponsored to compare different methods of teaching reading. People working on those projects pointed out that methods "given the same label were often not the same" (Stauffer, 1967, p. 563). There is a big need to crawl out from under labels. Solving this methodological problem brings us back to aspects of exposing the "stuff" of instructional interventions.

The political problems of investigating the influence of whole language on children's literacy development jump out of the pages of the November 1990 issue of *Educational Researcher*. In that volume, McKenna, Robinson, and Miller offered what I saw as a sincere attempt to describe a research agenda for coming to understand the effects of whole language on the acquisition of literacy. They offered that, in this research, "the instrumentation by which effectiveness is measured in reading (will be) the single most important cause for concern" (p. 5). Moreover, they asserted the need for those in the movement to be involved in determining the instrumentation and for the use of quantitative and qualitative methods. Although these suggestions were rejected outright by one proponent of the movement (Edelsky, 1990), the authors subsequently suggested that "others within the whole-language community are more receptive to the sort of collaboration we have proposed" (p. 13).

McKenna, Robinson, and Miller's suggestions are a good place to start to figure out how to conduct research on the influence of the whole-language movement on children's acquisition of reading and related literacy and evaluate its effectiveness. As this work proceeds, it will be especially important that the effects of whole language on, for lack of a better term, *at-risk* children, many of whom are poor and of a minority, be most seriously considered.

RECOMMENDATIONS

Reading research has allowed much to be learned about one of the most complex endeavors in which people engage, but much remains to be learned. Before summarizing the recommendations that I offered here, I want briefly to reflect on the complexity of the process—which is so easy for many of us and so difficult for others.

It is commonplace for reading researchers to fold into their introductions to articles and reports some version of the phrase: "Reading is a complex cognitive process." When other reading researchers encounter that phrase, it touches the tip of an iceberg of information about what it takes to engage in a complex cognitive process. But most adult competent readers, including teachers, do not fully appreciate that reading is a very complex human endeavor. Just and Carpenter (1987) discussed why those who engage easily in the reading process tend not to be aware of what an "intellectual feat" reading is:

> An expert can make a complex skill look easy. But the apparent effortlessness of a chess master or concert pianist does not deceive us. What we sometimes fail to appreciate is that skilled reading is an intellectual feat no less complex than chess playing. Readers of this (paper) are, in many ways, as expert at reading as chess masters are expert at chess. But because of the deceptively effortless look and feel of reading, and the fact that there are relatively many "reading masters" in our society, reading skill is not given as much credit for complexity as other forms of expertise. Its complexity is also one reason why not everyone learns to read, and certainly not everyone becomes an expert reader. (p. 3)

As we mount the kind of research I recommended, we must direct our attention toward those who do not learn to read easily; often these are poor and minority children whose very survival as adults may depend on their having developed this competence. We must also direct attention to analyses of higher levels of literacy—that is, learning and thinking from and about extended, complex, multiple-text presentations. To reiterate, I offer the following as appropriate next steps toward these overarching goals and toward the continuance of the fine-grained analyses that made the 1970s and 1980s so productive for the field:

• Continue theoretically driven and research-based descriptive analyses of school curricular materials.

• Pursue research on learning, over time, from extended complex texts. In this regard, it should be noted that although comprehension is a necessary condition, it is not a sufficient condition for learning from text.

• Continue both cognitive and motivational work on developing techniques to encourage students' active engagement with text.

• Support long-term engineering of instructional studies.

• Make the research instrumentation more widely available that will shed light on the rationale for innovations in practice and develop mechanisms for easy archival retrieval, so practitioners and the interested public can assess the quality of, and better implement practices based on, advanced knowledge of reading.

• Undertake the development of multiperspective models of the acquisition of reading.

• Pursue research, particularly training studies, on the role of phonemic awareness on the acquisition of reading.

• Pursue research on the role of writing in the acquisition of reading.

• Undertake research that allows the field to understand the impact of whole-language approaches on children's acquisition of reading and related literacy and to evaluate their effectiveness.

REFERENCES

Adams, M. J. (1990). *Beginning to read: Thinking and learning about print*. Cambridge, MA: The MIT Press.

Anderson, R. C., & Davison, A. (1988). Conceptual and empirical bases of readability formulas. In A. Davison & G. M. Green (Eds.), *Linguistic complexity and text comprehension: Readability issues reconsidered* (pp. 23–53). Hillsdale, NJ: Lawrence Erlbaum Associates.

Anderson, T. H., & Armbruster, B. B. (1984). Content area textbooks. In R. C. Anderson, J. Osborn, & R. J. Tierney (Eds.), *Learning to read in American schools* (pp. 193–224). Hillsdale, NJ: Lawrence Erlbaum Associates.

Anderson, R. C., Hiebert, E. H., Scott, J. A., & Wilkinson, I. A. G. (1985). *Becoming a nation of readers: The report of the Commission on Reading*. Washington, DC: U.S. Department of Education, National Institute of Education.

Au, K. H., & Kawakami, A. J. (1984). Vygotskian perspectives on discussion processes in small-group reading lessons. In P. L. Peterson, L. C. Wilkinson, & M. Hallinan (Eds.), *The social context of instruction* (pp. 209–225). Orlando, FL: Academic Press.

Ball, D. L., & Feiman-Nemser, S. (1988). Using textbooks and teachers' guides: A dilemma for beginning teachers and teacher educators. *Curriculum Inquiry, 18*, 401–423.

Barr, R. (1989). The social organization of literacy instruction. In S. McCormick & J. Zutell (Eds.), *Cognitive and social perspectives for literacy research and instruction: Thirty-eighth yearbook of the National Reading Conference* (pp. 19–33). Chicago, IL: National Reading Conference.

Beck, I. L., McKeown, M. G., Omanson, R. C., & Pople, M. T. (1984). Improving the comprehensibility of stories: The effects of revisions that improve coherence. *Reading Research Quarterly, 19*(3), 263–277.

Beck, I. L., McKeown, M. G., Sinatra, G. M., & Loxterman, J. A. (1991). Revising social studies text from a text-processing perspective: Evidence of improved comprehensibility. *Reading Research Quarterly 26*, 251–276.

Beck, I. L., Omanson, R. C., & McKeown, M. G. (1982). An instructional redesign of reading lessons: Effects on comprehension. *Reading Research Quarterly, 17,* 462–481.

Bloome, D., & Green, J. (1984). Directions in the sociolinguistic study of reading. In P. D. Pearson (Ed.), *Handbook of reading research* (pp. 395–421). New York: Longman.

Bossert, S. T. (1988–1989). Cooperative activities in the classroom. In E. Z. Rothkopf (Ed.), *Review of research in education* (Vol. 15, pp. 225–250). Washington, DC: American Educational Research Association.

Brown, J. S., Collins, A., & Duguid, P. (1989). Situated cognition and the culture of learning. *Educational Researcher, 18,* 32–43.

Brown, A. L., & Palincsar, A. S. (1982). Inducing strategic learning from texts by means of informed, self-control training. *Topics in learning and learning disabilities, 2*(1), 1–17.

Brown, A. L., & Palincsar, A. S. (1989). Guided, cooperative learning and individual knowledge acquisition. In L. B. Resnick (Ed.), *Knowing, learning, and instruction: Essays in honor of Robert Glaser* (pp. 393–451). Hillsdale, NJ: Lawrence Erlbaum Associates.

Bruner, J. S. (1957). Going beyond the information given. In H. Gruber (Ed.), *Contemporary approaches to cognition: A Symposium held at the University of Colorado* (pp. 41–70). Cambridge, MA: Harvard University Press.

Cazden, C. (1986). Classroom discourse. In M. C. Wittrock (Ed.), *Handbook of research on teaching* (3rd ed., pp. 432–462). New York: Macmillan.

Clay, M. M. (1966). *Emergent reading behavior.* Unpublished doctoral dissertation, University of Auckland, New Zealand.

Edelsky, C. (1990). Whose agenda is this anyway? A response to McKenna, Robinson, and Miller. *Educational Researcher, 19*(8), 7–11.

Ehri, L. C. (1978). Beginning reading from a psycholinguistic perspective: Amalgamation of word identities. In F. B. Murray (Ed.), *The development of the reading process* (pp. 1–33). Newark, DE: International Reading Association.

Ehri, L. C. (1991). Development of the ability to read words. In R. Barr, M. L. Kamil, P. B. Mosenthal, & P. D. Pearson (Eds.), *Handbook of reading research* (Vol. 2, pp. 383–417). White Plains, NY: Longman.

Frederiksen, C. H. (1975). Representing logical and semantic structure of knowledge acquired from discourse. *Cognitive Psychology, 7,* 371–458.

Gardner, H. (1985). *The mind's new science: A history of the cognitive revolution.* New York: Basic.

Goodman, K. S. (1976). Reading: A psycholinguistic guessing game. In H. Singer & R. Ruddell (Eds.), *Theoretical models and processes of reading* (pp. 497–508). Newark, DE: International Reading Association. (Original work published 1970)

Heath, S. B. (1991). The sense of being literate: Historical and cross-cultural features. In R. Barr, M. L. Kamil, P. B. Mosenthal, & P. D. Pearson (Eds.), *Handbook of reading research* (Vol. 2, pp. 3–25). White Plains, NY: Longman.

Hoffman, J. V. (1991). Teacher and school effects in learning to read. In R. Barr, M. L. Kamil, P. B. Mosenthal, & P. D. Pearson (Eds.), *Handbook of reading research* (Vol. 2, pp. 911–950). White Plains, NY: Longman.

Johnson, D. W., Maruyama, G., Johnson, R., Nelson, D., & Skon, L. (1981). Effects of cooperative, competitive, and individualistic goal structures on achievement: A meta-analysis. *Psychological Bulletin, 89,* 47–62.

Juel, C. (1991). Beginning reading. In R. Barr, M. L. Kamil, P. B. Mosenthal, & P. D. Pearson (Eds.), *Handbook of reading research* (Vol. 2, pp. 759–788). White Plains, NY: Longman.

Just, M. A., & Carpenter, P. A. (1987). *The psychology of reading and language comprehension.* Boston, MA: Allyn & Bacon.

Kintsch, W. (1974). *The representation of meaning in memory.* Hillsdale, NJ: Lawrence Erlbaum Associates.

Kintsch, W., & Vipond, D. (1979). Reading comprehension and readability in educational practice and psychological theory. In L. G. Nilson (Ed.), *Perspectives on memory research* (pp. 325–365). Hillsdale, NJ: Lawrence Erlbaum Associates.

Lundberg, I., Frost, J., & Peterson, O. (1988). Effects of an extensive program for stimulating phonological awareness in preschool children. *Reading Research Quar-*

terly, 23, 263–284.

Mandler, J. M., & Johnson, N. S. (1977). Remembrance of things parsed: Story structure and recall. *Cognitive Psychology, 9,* 111–151.

McKenna, M. C., Robinson, R. D., & Miller, J. W. (1990). Whole language: A research agenda for the nineties. *Educational Researcher, 19*(8), 3–6.

Meyer, B. J. F. (1975). *The organization of prose and its effect on memory.* Amsterdam: North Holland.

Miller, G. A. (1965). Some preliminaries to psycholinguistics. *American Psychologist, 20,* 15–20.

O'Flahavan, J. O. (1989). *Second graders' social, intellectual, and affective development in varied group discussions about narrative texts: An explanation of participation structures.* Unpublished doctoral dissertation, University of Illinois, Urbana-Champaign.

Palincsar, A. S., & Brown, A. L. (1984). Reciprocal teaching of comprehension-fostering and monitoring activities. *Cognition and Instruction, 1*(2), 117–175.

Paris, S. G., Cross, D. R., & Lipson, M.Y. (1984). Informed strategies for learning: A program to improve children's awareness and comprehension. *Journal of Educational Psychology, 76,* 1239–1252.

Pearson, P. D. (1989). Reading the whole language movement. *The Elementary School Journal, 90,* 231–241.

Pearson, P. D., & Fielding, L. (1991). Comprehension instruction. In R. Barr, M. L. Kamil, P. B. Mosenthal, & P. D. Pearson (Eds.), *Handbook of reading research* (Vol. 2, pp. 815–860). White Plains, NY: Longman.

Perfetti, C. A. (1985). *Reading ability.* New York: Oxford University Press.

Pinnell, G. S. (1989). Reading recovery: Helping at-risk children learn to read. *The Elementary School Journal, 90,* 161–183.

Resnick, L. B. (1987). Learning in school and out. *Educational Researcher, 16*(9), 13–20.

Resnick, L. B. (Ed.). (1989). *Knowing, learning, and instruction: Essays in honor of Robert Glaser.* Hillsdale, NJ: Lawrence Erlbaum Associates.

Rumelhart, D. E. (1975). Notes on a schema for stories. In D. G. Brown & A. Collins (Eds.), *Representation and understanding: Studies in cognitive science* (pp. 211–236). New York: Academic Press.

Rumelhart, D. E. (1977). Toward an interactive model of reading. In S. Dornic (Ed.), *Attention and performance: Proceedings of the sixth international symposium on attention and performance* (Vol. 6, pp. 573–603). Hillsdale, NJ: Lawrence Erlbaum Associates.

Shantz, C. U. (Ed.). (1987, July). Children's reading and the development of phonological awareness (Invitational issue). *Merrill-Palmer Quarterly: Journal of Developmental Psychology, 33*(3).

Sharan, S. (1980). Cooperative learning in small groups: Recent methods and effects on achievement, attitudes, and ethnic relations. *Review of Educational Research, 50,* 241–271.

Slavin, R. E. (1989). Cooperative learning and student achievement. In R. E. Slavin (Ed.), *School and classroom organization* (pp. 129–156). Hillsdale, NJ: Lawrence Erlbaum Associates.

Stanovich, K. E. (1980). Toward an interactive compensatory model of individual differences in the development of reading fluency. *Reading Research Quarterly, 16,* 32–71.

Stanovich, K. E. (1991). Word recognition: Changing perspectives. In R. Barr, M. L. Kamil, P. B. Mosenthal, & P. D. Pearson (Eds.), *Handbook of reading research* (Vol. 2, pp. 418–452). White Plains, NY: Longman.

Stauffer, R. G. (Ed.). (1967). *The first grade reading studies: Findings of individual investigations.* Newark, DE: International Reading Association.

Stein, N. L., & Glenn, C. G. (1979). An analysis of story comprehension in elementary school children. In R. O. Freedle (Ed.), *Advances in discourse processing: Vol. 2. New directions in discourse processing* (pp. 53–120). Norwood, NJ: Ablex.

Sulzby, E., & Teale, W. (1991). Emergent literacy. In R. Barr, M. L. Kamil, P. B. Mosenthal, & P. D. Pearson (Eds.), *Handbook of reading research* (Vol. 2, pp. 727–758). White Plains, NY: Longman.

Trabasso, T., Secco, T., & van den Broek, P. (1984). Causal cohesion and story coherence. In H. Mandl, N. L. Stein, & T. Trabasso (Eds.), *Learning and comprehension of text* (pp. 83–111). Hillsdale, NJ: Lawrence Erlbaum Associates.

Vellutino, F. R., & Denckla, M. B. (1991). Cognitive and neuropsychological foundations of word identification in poor and normally developing readers. In R. Barr, M. L. Kamil, P. B. Mosenthal, & P. D. Pearson (Eds.), *Handbook of reading research* (Vol. 2, pp. 571–608). White Plains, NY: Longman.

Vygotsky, L. S. (1978). *Mind in society: The development of higher psychological processes* (M. Cole, V. John-Steiner, S. Scribner, & E. Souberman, Eds.). Cambridge, MA: Harvard University Press.

Watson, D. J. (1989). Defining and describing whole language. *The Elementary School Journal, 90,* 129–141.

Weinstein, C. S. (1991). The classroom as a social context for learning. In M. R. Rosenzweig & L. W. Porter (Eds.), *Annual review of psychology* (Vol. 42, pp. 493–525). Palo Alto, CA: Annual Reviews.

Wixson, K. K., & Lipson, M. Y. (1991). Perspectives on reading disability research. In R. Barr, M. L. Kamil, P. B. Mosenthal, & P. D. Pearson (Eds.), *Handbook of reading research* (Vol. 2, pp. 539–570). White Plains, NY: Longman.

5

Research and Practice:
A Practitioner's View

Joy N. Monahan
Reading Consultant, Orange County Public Schools
Orlando, Florida

More than 65 years of reading research summaries! That is what educators have within reach to guide curriculum and instruction to create schools of excellence for the decade of the 1990s. Do we need additional research? Do we need different kinds of research? Do we need better ways of disseminating information to teachers and supporting their use of research findings?

I believe the answer to those questions is "yes" as I think of the diversified needs in education today. When we look at the changes that are rapid and constant in our society, we realize it has been several years since the basic research on schema and metacognition. Certainly there is little research on middle or secondary reading problems. The rapidly growing number of students with limited English proficiency point to culturally diversified research needs. Given that the national goals emphasize heavy school-based decision making, research evaluating the effectiveness of this model is needed. Other key areas within easy sight for researchers are the many tangents related to technology, productive professional development for teachers in the field, and effective assessment and its uses. As the brain-based learning information multiplies, studies on its implementation need to find their way to classroom teachers as they continue to find better ways to teach effectively.

WHAT HAVE WE LEARNED?

Past research has informed current practice. Teachers today know more about how students acquire literacy skills, and how to develop and encourage these skills. We know more about how the mind works to construct meaning and organize information. Enhancing comprehension—not drill in isolated reading and study skills—has become the ultimate goal of reading. These advances in our understandings of what reading is and how to teach students most effectively to get meaning from print, coupled with the technological revolution, make this an exciting time to be a reading educator. I believe that research in five key areas has been particularly influential:

- Cognition/metacognition.
- Prior knowledge.
- Reading as an active process.
- Text organization and considerateness.
- Instructional techniques that develop good readers.

Cognition/Metacognition

Cognitive psychologists have enhanced our understanding of what students know about how they learn (cognition), their self-awareness of reading and learning problems (metacognition), and subsequent methods to solve those problems. When good readers become conscious of their thinking and comprehension, they can deliberately try different strategies when comprehension breaks down. Effective readers are those who monitor their own understanding while reading, being constantly alert to comprehension failure. Students who are not aware of thinking and problem-solving processes must be taught how to search actively for meaning from texts.

Prior Knowledge

Background knowledge, experience, purpose, and setting influence what the reader gains from the text. Research that focused on the reader and what that reader brings to the text showed us that the reader's familiarity with the topic, interest in, and reason for reading all influence what is understood from the text. The more prior knowledge a student has about the subject and the better he or she understands the purpose for reading it, the more the student will gain from reading. Students must be taught to activate prior knowledge, to set purposes and to predict before reading, and to search for ways that the text relates to what is already known and to what in the text helps answer a reader's needs in reading.

Reading as an Active Process

Today, reading programs are experiencing a period of transition—a deliberate and significant change—caused by the impact of the research on comprehension and metacognition by the cognitive psychologists during the past 10 to 15 years. Instead of workbook drills on isolated reading and study skills, emphasis is placed on teaching strategies that promote interactive reading and learning in content area assignments as well as in reading classes. This process model of reading stresses comprehension and the interactive nature of reading. Reading is treated as a process of the student's interacting with print, and bridging the gap between what is known and what is new. The process model of reading emphasizes:

- Constructing meaning from print.
- Applying strategies to learn from text.
- Developing expertise through practice.
- Preparing students to read for the life-long pursuit of learning and pleasure.

Reading becomes a thinking–reasoning process used before, during, and after lessons, rather than a series of sequential skills (Palincsar et al., 1985).

Text Organization and Considerateness

Research into the fourth area, textbook considerateness, revealed *how* the material is presented influences comprehension. "Considerateness" encompasses organization and structure of the text, concept explanations, clarity and coherence of topics, appropriateness for students and accurateness and consistency of information (Armbruster, 1987; Armbruster & Anderson, 1984).

The familiar old model of reading suggests that reading primarily consists of acquiring various subskills in a sequential fashion. The reader proceeds to unlock sounds letter by letter, then words and sentences, which automatically produce comprehension. However, with the cognition model, readers first activate background knowledge to construct meaning. Using a metaphor of a road map or a set of blueprints to describe this process of reading when trying to comprehend text helps students perceive their active learning mode. However, even considerate texts may not be enough to assure comprehension. Students may have ideas and experiences that get in the way of new learning. As teachers recognize the constructivist aspect of the readers' task, they must encompass in their instruction factors such as the students' prior knowledge, the context, and the students' repertoire of learning strategies.

Instructional Techniques that Develop Good Readers

We have learned that teachers need to provide direct instruction in techniques to help students become good readers. Comprehension of information is easier if students are instructed in strategies that cause them to focus their attention on relevant information, synthesize the information, and integrate it with what they already know. Direct instruction in comprehension means explaining the steps in a thought process that give birth to comprehension. It may mean that the teacher models a strategy by thinking aloud about how he or she personally is going about understanding a passage. The instruction includes not only information on *how* to use the strategy but also the rationale for *why* and *when* to use the strategy. Instruction of this type is the surest means of developing the strategic processing that is a characteristic of skilled readers (Pearson, 1985; Vygotsky, 1962).

This type of instruction needs reinforcement during the student's entire day in every area of study. *Becoming a Nation of Readers* (Anderson, Hiebert, Scott, & Wilkinson, 1985) stated that "the most logical place for instruction in most reading and thinking strategies is in social studies and science, rather than in separate lessons about reading. The reason is the strategies are useful mainly when the student is grappling with important but unfamiliar content" (p. 73). In education, the idea that reading instruction and subject matter instruction should be integrated is an old one, but there is little indication that such integration occurs often in practice.

RESEARCH PRIORITIES FOR THE FUTURE

These five factors have provided a strong focus for the current state of the art in reading instruction. Given this base, what are the critical areas for future research? Thinking of priorities for reading research into the year 2000 is an exciting experience. Many areas are worthy of consideration. However, I believe that research needs to address four key areas:

- Students in middle and senior high schools.
- Ethnographic research conducted by teachers.
- Support for professional growth for teachers.
- Making current research information more widely available, and more useful.

Students in Middle and Senior High School

Most reading research has focused on the elementary grades. Additional attention needs to be paid to instruction in middle and secondary school, where strong disillusionment creates dropout fever. Reading instruction at all levels must relate to the increasing demands encountered by the learner. As students progress through the grades, the focus shifts from learning to read to reading to learn. Most of the reading tasks at the middle and secondary level involve expository textbook material, which requires students to learn many abstract concepts in the space of a few pages; therefore, instruction that reflects attention to each of the five key areas that I summarized in my introduction is paramount.

What particular additional foci do I suggest? Again, selection is difficult, but I believe that attention should be paid to the following areas.

Cooperative Learning

Using cooperative grouping techniques along with learning strategy suggestions makes a powerful combination for helping the high-risk learners who are among the major concerns of educators today. This blending of teaching practices helps meet the four needs of teenagers that Glasser (Gough, 1987) cited—love, belonging, power, and fun. Glasser said that teachers cannot make students learn, but they can set things up so that students want to learn. When the learners' needs are more closely met they will think school is a place where they want to learn and to work. Teachers providing effective instruction create a feeling of self-worth and increase student learning and remembering. What better goals can educators select when preparing future citizens to function constructively and be able to participate as knowledgeable decisionmakers and independent learners?

The Effects of a Changing World

The world in which students live is changing, and the students in our classes are more diverse. Educators need to heed advice from Hodgkinson (1988): "We can't plan schools and curriculum for tomorrow without thinking hard about the kids we're planning for" (p. 25). The major issue of how America will compete successfully as a world power is moving toward workplace literacy, productivity, and quality. Sound and researched ways of making sure students have learned how to learn, how to think, and how to solve social and philosophical problems will be needed as new disciplines for a high-tech society come into place.

Parental Involvement

Parental involvement's benefits have been clearly documented. The Carnegie Council on Adolescent Development's (1989) *Turning Points* stated: "By middle grades, the home–school connection has been significantly reduced, and in some cases is nonexistent" (p. 66). Efforts to reinvolve parents in meaningful roles, keeping them informed, and offering opportunities to learn about helping students at home and at school pay off at senior high as well as at middle school levels—but we need to find more effective ways of reaching and involving them.

Research by Teachers

Traditionally, research has been conducted by universities or federally funded research laboratories. However, a new movement of even as great significance as university-based research is the current teacher-as-researcher activities. It is this teacher-as-researcher movement that merits a priority in the OERI research agenda into the year 2000. A resolution adopted by the Board of Directors of the International Reading Association (1988) stated:

> Instructional decisions are best made by teachers who conduct research in their own classrooms. They analyze the performance of their students. The classroom becomes a collaborative community of literacy research where teachers and their students have permission to reflect, analyze and problem-solve about instruction. (p. 1)

The promising avenue of naturalistic research for improving the teaching and learning processes in the classroom makes the concept of teacher-as-researcher more viable. *Naturalistic research* (Olson, 1990) is a methodology that precludes the use of exotic research designs and complicated statistical procedures—procedures that are impossible for the individual classroom teacher to implement. However, it helps teachers observe and interpret how students in their classrooms construct meaning as they do or do not learn and remember. Olson stated that: "Teachers involved in naturalistic studies document the ways they teach and the ways their children learn in the classroom, learning about themselves as well as their students" (p. 13).

Neilsen (1990) wrote about teacher researchers informing teaching, stimulating professional growth, and influencing colleagues to investigate their own practices. This research requires a questioning stance, a willingness to see, and a reflexive teaching mode, one in which theory and practice propel one another. Neilsen goes on to ask, "And what counts as research?" She answered:

> Teachers, alone and in collaboration with other researchers, are conducting experimental studies, engaging in naturalistic inquiry, and participating in action research and in critical research. Are the results gained through manipulation of variables and reported in statistical terms any more or any less useful to the profession or to the teacher than the results of surveys, transcripts of interviews, or insights gained from a practiced eye? In its many forms, teacher research is providing the reading and writing field with different voices and other ways of seeing. The interest is growing rapidly, and reports of classroom research appear regularly in professional journals and at conferences. Teachers are seeking out one another to explore, collaborate, debate, and stimulate further work. (p. 12)

Patterson, Stansell, and Lee (1990) stated that "the most powerful data about instruction come from authentic learning situations in real classrooms." They applaud the power that comes to teachers when they do research because it changes their teaching in significant ways and teachers grow professionally as their beliefs and theories about learning evolve. Harste (1990) stated that "If successful, the movement should result in teachers and children being in charge of the profession instead of theorists, university researchers, administrators, basal authors and others who rarely, if ever, come in contact with children."

Teacher-researcher options can range from formal, where they may plan simple experimental studies conducted in one or two classrooms for evaluating teaching strategies, to informal, where teachers and students become a community of learners, perhaps observing, in a self-research style, their own teaching or learning using writing or teaching logs. Teacher-researchers may focus on new ideas or just reexamine old approaches, as one group of teachers did when they observed that round-robin oral reading dominated social studies instruction in many classrooms. They noted that instruction began with the teacher discussing the upcoming topic followed by oral reading in turn-taking fashion. While awaiting their turn to read, all students supposedly followed along in their text. Teachers posed mostly literal level questions and students parroted answers. Knowing that old habits die hard, they did a study to examine alternatives.

In this teacher research, the control class brainstormed about their lesson topic before reading silently, and then they read orally in round-robin style with discussion, now and then, led by the teacher. The experimental group also brainstormed but continued using their brainstormed background information to categorize main ideas and details about their topic of study. As they read the lesson, they added information to their main idea and detail chart. When the two groups took the same test over the information studied, the experimental class did considerably better. Later they reversed the classes and repeated the experiment using another chapter. The same results held, convincing both teachers and students that more learning occurred from the brainstorming followed by charting the ideas and writing them down in relationship patterns than from the round-robin routine. Teacher research can be a powerful influence for changing instruction.

A high school geometry teacher combined key vocabulary with brainstorming about meanings of the words, followed by his writing a summary of students' comments on the chalkboard, together with clarified misconceptions. Before reading the lesson silently, students listed two or three ideas they hoped to gain from the selection, after which they practiced doing sample problems following discussion and rereading. When 31% of the experimental geometry students did better than their control group, the geometry teacher became convinced of the importance of setting the stage before students read the assignment. In related teacher research, high school biology and history students learned more content when taking notes in a two-column style by which they could study daily and review effectively for test times, than with reading and rereading their text.

Teacher research revitalizes both teachers and students as it promotes reflective teaching and learning. It provides a connection between instructional methods and results and helps teachers apply research findings to their own classrooms.

The teacher-as-researcher movement may help solve a problem noted by Banach (1991): School districts often miss the boat because they take too long gearing up for change. He stressed the need for a vision and a process for change with a plan, one with ownership and support. The movement of teachers-as-researchers at the grassroot level seems to fulfill most of Banach's essentials for change. Prevalent in the teacher-as-researcher movement is the notion that students become active learners much the same as the idea of the student-as-worker portrayed in the credo of Ted Sizer's *Coalition of Essential Schools.*

The following areas are profitable for teacher-as-researcher activities.

Helping Students Become Strategic Readers

We need additional research on how to help students become strategic readers. Cognitive researchers showed that good readers have specific strategies that they use when their understanding breaks down during reading, strategies related to knowing why they were reading and to devoting their complete attention to the task of reading. Good readers are aware of what they are doing and constantly monitoring their understanding (Brown, 1982). Further research indicated that strategic reading improves achievement, and it can be taught (Paris, 1985; Paris, Lipson, & Wilson, 1983).

Teacher Researchers

Teacher researchers, because they work with students every day, are in the best position to refine this work and to develop better ways to provide students with training in how to activate background knowledge, set the purpose for the reading task, and check on understanding that helps produce strategic readers. This work is particularly important for poor readers, who often do not know there is a message to be understood in a passage or what steps they need to take to understand it.

Examples of strategies for learning and remembering that make excellent topics about which teachers might do research concerning students' learning outcomes are: predicting, activating background knowledge, self-monitoring, organizing information, interacting, summarizing, and clarifying.

More Effective Use of Technology

Change is usually a slow process until technology in education is the topic. Here change is occurring constantly, and falling prices for technological tools allowed an increasing, although still small, number of schools to become completely equipped with computers, laser discs and players, video camcorders, satellite dishes and system networks. Technologically linking people with the power of video, as through a teleconference, has sociological, educational, and emotional effects for the participants. Multimedia interactive instruction helps keep learners actively at work. Students and teachers can create documents that include words as well as images, animations, and video clips. Presentations can be viewed by thousands, modeling can be shown, and panel discussions can provide reactions and critiques.

The research focus should be on developing or refining instructional strategies that involve teaching as thinking and on restructuring efforts proven to increase student achievement. Research on learning how to learn, rather than learning specific facts, will be helped through focusing on development and applications with optical scanners,

CD-ROM, videodisks, and modems; finding better ways to train teachers to use these electronic aids will be a high priority. Worthwhile staff development of a practical nature will be vital to this electronic teaching power. Presentations must include how to move from the "real" to the "ideal," and involve techniques such as role-playing, which helps teachers apply the information and skills presented.

Interdisciplinary Instruction

Attempts to reduce the fragmentation of thinking and learning in middle and high schools are alleviated by interdisciplinary teaching. Interdisciplinary teaching can be in a classroom with one teacher relating problem solving and learning to many disciplines—thus illustrating the interconnectedness of the curriculum—or it can be with a team using cooperative planning and common-themed units to portray commonalities and interrelatedness of learnings in different subject areas. Still another approach could be an entire school devoting energies to enhancing vocabulary instruction through concept development and ownership of words through meaningful contexts related to the students' own experiences. Additional research may show which approaches are most appropriate for different schools and students.

Reading and Writing Connection

Research on how to encourage greater integration of reading, language arts, listening, and writing seems necessary, particularly across the curriculum in content area classes. Recent research confirms the interrelationships between reading and writing, but more studies need to be encouraged, particularly in content areas at the middle and high school levels. Students need opportunities to write beyond the English classroom. Responding to what is read or learned from a lesson encourages students to generate ideas and to receive valuable feedback on the quality of their thinking. It is alarming to hear how little time some students actually spend in the composing and comprehending process. Applebee (cited in Squire, 1983, p. 581) reported that "only four percent of social studies and science teachers in grades seven through twelve" incorporate writing into their disciplines. This alarming finding is evidenced by the recent poor results on standardized tests when students are required to answer inferential thinking questions or to generate a written summary on a reading passage (Tierney, Readence, & Dishner, 1985).

Promising avenues of research include how to tailor students' academic journals to many purposes, from monitoring the learning-thinking process to enhancing personal writing production. Fulwiler (1991) wrote about journal assignments that can be used to introduce a lesson with a 5-minute journal-write predicting from their background knowledge what the author will reveal about the topic of study. An end of class, journal-write summarizes learnings and provides a springboard for follow-up activities, or might be used during the lesson to pause and reflect on an idea or problem. Research exploring ideas such as these and other reading–writing relationships needs to be developed.

Authentic Assessment: Portfolios

Increased attention to authentic assessment and the importance of adding it to the evaluation of students' learning through portfolios, essays, and open-ended questions increase the need to provide teachers with additional information on how to use these new assessments. Alternative assessments such as portfolios can present a continuous picture of what is being accomplished in actual classroom experiences as well as reveal what a student can actually do with his or her learning. Principal Susan Akroyd (1991) stated that, "Portfolios can help reform schools because they integrally involve teachers, parents, students, and administrators in analyzing present performance as well as encouraging future growth" (p. 1). Using portfolios as a supplement to report cards is valuable as teachers and students select the best pieces of work and make comments on why each piece was chosen.

Because of the potential impact of portfolios and other authentic assessment methodologies on the classroom, teacher researchers must play a primary role in their refinement. Tierney, Carter, and Desai (1991) provided excellent help for teachers getting started with portfolios and sustaining them, and also discussed helping students become self-evaluators of the quality of their work. These ideas make excellent teacher-as-researcher projects.

Strengthened and Enhanced Staff Development

Joyce and Showers (1988) reminded us that knowledge about innovation in education, the conduct of curricular change, and the processes by which educators learn new skills and knowledge and how to use them, have made great progress in the past decade. They described the need for staff development to help educators as they work with students and what they bring to the school context as they promote learning, thinking, and remembering, in the culture that education has developed. They say staff development increases the ability of teachers to engage in that competition.

Research is vital that will provide information on the effects of providing time for teachers and administrators to participate in staff development, as well as the types of staff development activities that are most effective. Staff development sessions are a must to help administrators and teachers deal with the rapid change in the use of technology awareness and practice toward efficiency. As more and more community and business leaders as well as parents are overseeing school budgets and setting curricula, having an adequate knowledge base about schooling effectiveness will become paramount for these active participants.

Dissemination of What Works

Research and data for *Becoming a Nation of Readers* (Anderson et al., 1985) was gathered almost a decade ago. Much new information has been discovered since that time. It seems the time is right for a new national statement on Reading for Excellence that would serve to support President Bush and the National Governor's Association's six educational goals. When middle and high schools pursue excellence to improve students' achievement, there are some key factors that research could help support. There are many sources of information, including a flip chart developed by the International Reading Association (Monahan & Hinson, 1988). Others can be found in the *Handbook of Reading Research* (Barr, Kamil, Mosenthal, & Pearson, 1991) and the *Handbook on Teaching the English Language Arts* (Flood, Jensen, Lapp, & Squire, 1991). These findings need to be packaged in a variety of formats and disseminated widely.

A blue ribbon quality middle and secondary reading program needs to be based on research evidence. Areas where teachers need information on effective programs and practices—particularly on those developed by teacher researchers include:

- How to set goals and objectives.
- How to budget for teacher interaction development and adaptation of curriculum materials.
- How to provide ongoing staff development training in reading, including such ideas as demonstrating, modeling, coaching, and feedback.
- How to make effective use of assessment and evaluation data.
- How to conduct action research by teachers, schoolwide, or in collaboration with a university.
- How to study and apply current research.

- How to establish a reading committee.
- How to promote public relations through such vehicles as newsletters, "research notes," and parents' information sheets.
- How to promote reading for pleasure.
- How to best employ a reading resource specialist to implement, update, and promote the reading effort.
- How to provide administrators and faculty with current knowledge about reading trends, issues, and research.

SUMMARY

Thinking of priorities for reading research into the year 2000 is an exciting experience. How to teach complex concepts to all students—at-risk, minorities, disadvantaged, culturally diverse, and gifted—would be a stellar attainment. Professional growth and development of teachers occur as they tackle those tasks plus learning to use the marvelous world of technology to the best advantage while accomplishing success. The ethnographic research and the newer movement of teachers as researchers offers promise of school-based evidence that may thrive in the days of restructuring and national goal achievement. Much sound reading research is out there now, but making it readily available to all—particularly those in the remote areas—is an objective that can be supported by research activities.

The ways in which the reading research agenda serve to disseminate that knowledge—the knowledge that *Becoming a Nation of Readers* (Anderson et al., 1985) told us is now available to make worthwhile improvements in reading throughout the United States. In order for this to occur, the classroom practices of the best teachers in the best schools need to be introduced everywhere, so the improvements in reading would be dramatic.

REFERENCES

Akroyd, P. S. (1991). Portfolios: A "cultural awareness." *Elementary Language Arts Communique,* *1*(1), 1–2.

Anderson, R. C., Hiebert, E. H., Scott, J. A., & Wilkinson, I. A. G. (1985). *Becoming a nation of readers: The report of the commission on reading* (Contract No. 400-83-0057). Washington, DC: National Institute of Education.

Armbruster, B. B. (1987, May). *What features in textbooks help children learn?* Preconvention institute conducted at the 32nd annual convention of the International Reading Association, Anaheim, CA.

Armbruster, B. B., & Anderson, T. H. (1984). Content area. textbooks. In R. C. Anderson, J. Osborn, & R. J. Tierney (Eds.), *Learning to read in American schools: Basal readers and content texts* (pp. 193–226). Hillsdale, NJ: Lawrence Erlbaum Associates.

Banach, W. J. (1991). *The top ten educational issues (1991).* Warren, MI: The Institute for Future Studies at Macomb Community College.

Barr, R., Kamil, M. L., Mosenthal, P., & Pearson, P. D. (Eds.). (1991). *Handbook of reading research* (Vol. 2, pp. 68–96, 171–341, 383–724, 727–1013). New York: Longman.

Board of Directors. (1988). *Resolution*. Newark, DE: International Reading Association.

Brown, A. L. (1982). Learning how to learn from reading. In J. A. Langer & M. T. Smith-Burke (Eds.) *Reader meets author/bridging the gap* (pp. 26–54). Newark, DE: International Reading Association.

Carnegie Council on Adolescent Development. (1989). *Turning points: Preparing American youth for the 21st century*. New York: Carnegie Corporation of New York.

Flood, J., Jensen, J. M., Lapp, D., & Squire, J. R. (Eds.). (1991). *Handbook of research on teaching the English language arts*. (pp. 123–250, 259–422, 425–549, 559–843). New York: Macmillan.

Fulwiler, T. (1991). Student journals. In B. M. Power & R. Hubbard (Eds.), *Literacy in process: The Heinemann reader* (pp. 203–220). Portsmouth, NH: Heinemann.

Gough, P. (1987). The key to improving schools: An interview with William Glasser. *Phi Delta Kappan, 68*(9), 656–662.

Harste, J. C. (1990). Foreword. In M. W. Olson. (Ed.). *Opening the door to action research*. Newark, DE: International Reading Association.

Hodgkinson, H. (1988). The right schools for the right kids. *Educational Leadership, 45*(5), 10–14.

Joyce, B., & Showers, B. (1988). *Student achievement through staff development*. White Plains, NY: Longman.

Monahan, J., & Hinson, B. (1988). *New directions in reading instruction*. Newark, DE: International Reading Association.

Neilsen, L. (1990, February/March). Teachers as researchers: New visions. *Reading Today*, p. 12.

Olson, M. W. (Ed.). (1990). Opening the door to classroom research. *Reading Today*. Newark, DE: International Reading Association.

Olson, M. W. (1990, June/July). Teachers as researchers: Guidelines for research *Reading Today*, p. 13.

Palincsar, A. S., Ogle, D. S., Jones, B. F., Carr, E. G., & Ransom, K. (1985). *Facilitator's manual for teaching reading as thinking*. Washington, DC: Association for Supervision and Curriculum Development.

Paris, S. G. (1985). Using classroom dialogues and guided practice to teach comprehension strategies. In T. L. Harris & E. J. Cooper (Eds.), *Reading, thinking, and concept development* (pp. 133–146). New York: College Board Publications.

Paris, S. G., Lipson, M. Y., & Wilson, K. K. (1983). Becoming a strategic reader. *Contemporary Educational Psychology, 8*(3), 293–316.

Patterson, L., Stansell, J. C., & Lee, S. (1990). *Teacher research: From promise to power*. Katonah, NY: Richard C. Owen Publishers.

Pearson, P. D. (1985). Changing the face of reading comprehension instruction. *The Reading Teacher, 38*(8), 724–738.

Squire, J. R. (1983, May). Composing and comprehending: Two sides of the same basic process. *Language Arts*, p. 581.

Tierney, R. J., Carter, M. A., & Desai, L. E. (1991). *Portfolio assessment in the reading–writing classroom*. Norwood, MA: Christopher-Gordon Publishers.

Tierney, R. J., Readence, J. E., & Dishner, E. K. (1985). *Reading strategies and practices: A compendium (2nd Ed.)*. Boston, MA: Allyn & Bacon.

Vygotsky, L. S. (1962). *Thought and language*. Cambridge, MA: MIT Press.

6

A Reading Agenda for At-Risk Students: The Practitioner Speaks Out

Sara I. Scroggins
Literacy Consultant, St. Louis, Missouri

Reading in the year 2000 will prove to be quite a challenge to educators. Where are we going? This is the question we must ask ourselves as we move into this new decade. Schools will have children who are more culturally diverse, drug addicted, homeless, and products of single, teenage parents. Over the past 20 years, I have seen an entirely different student emerge because of changes in the family structure, constant family mobility, increased drug use, the abuse of technology (especially television), and the changing role of the teacher.

Being a teacher is a tremendous responsibility. Being a teacher of children who have been deemed "at risk" because of their economic status, family background, learning problems, ethnicity, and inner-city lifestyle is an even greater challenge. However, it is one that I have undertaken with great pride for the past 37 years. As a classroom teacher, reading specialist, and administrator in the urban schools, I understand too clearly what the reading problems of our children are, but I also realize that these problems can be overcome if we are willing to make the necessary changes in attitudes, instructional practices, and school environments.

A PURPOSEFUL READING AGENDA

Children in urban school settings can succeed in both reading and general learning if we care enough to offer them the same educational opportunities that children who are not at risk are offered on a *daily* basis. The reading agenda I propose in this chapter is based on my own experiences with these children and with the findings offered through the research literature that support my beliefs and instructional practices. Promoting daily reading, overcoming barriers to literacy, using diverse materials and teaching techniques, and including parents in the learning process are all part of the agenda.

In my estimation, sufficient research has been conducted on teaching methods, strategies, materials, school climate, effective teachers, racial groups' learning difficulties, and curriculum requirements for students. What we need now is to act on the research recommendations and to evaluate what really works over the long haul. We must move from what most classroom teachers view as the stagnation of conducting additional research and producing reports by blue ribbon committees to implementing effective educational practices. What most classroom teachers want to know is, "What can I do tomorrow to help my students read and learn?" To help them answer that question, we need to reexamine issues surrounding at-risk children, to understand the real causes of the problem, and to provide lasting solutions.

Dummet (1984) acknowledged that African-American, inner-city children as a group are not learning to read adequately. Even though national studies, such as the Reading Report Card and the National Assessment of Educational Progress, report that African-American children have improved, they still are behind White children in reading achievement. Reasons for this failure were attributed to language usage, family instability, children's experiential background, and the differences between family values and school practices. Each is addressed here with recommendations for educators.

Language usage, in many cases, identifies social status, ethnicity, and educational attainment. Many inner-city children do not use the standard English language recognized by educators who tend to embrace middle-class values.

A number of researchers addressed the problems associated with learners who speak a dialect that is different from standard English. Linda Christensen (1990) maintained that in our society, language classifies an individual, and children in the inner city are no exception to this classification or its consequences. Christensen revealed that one's grammar usage is an indication of both class and cultural background and maintained there is a bias against those who do not use language correctly. In her research on black dialect, Nancy Cecil (1988) discovered that teachers expected higher academic achievement, reading success, and intelligence from children who spoke standard English than from those who spoke African-American dialect. William O'Bruba (1986) stated that when children who speak an African-American dialect enter school, they discover that their language is unacceptable at best and openly rejected at worst. O'Bruba contended that before teachers can successfully teach children who speak black dialect, they must become sensitized to these children's problems and the kinds of environments that produced them.

One way reading teachers can help speakers of dialects is through the analysis of miscues that children make in oral reading. When listening to children read, the teacher needs to be aware of changes in the meaning of a written selection that children make, not in the pronunciation of words. The focus on reading instruction should be on a search for meaning, not just on accuracy of decoding words.

To help children move systematically in reading and writing from using dialect in oral language to reading standard English, I have used language experience stories. Language experience uses the actual language of the children in a nonthreatening manner. Using language experience activities helps teachers to understand and recognize the uniqueness of each of their students. When I have used children's stories and experiences, they were initially recorded in the actual language of the children. This was followed by several rereadings and rewritings in which the children were encouraged to incorporate standard English into the stories.

It is not enough to listen nonjudgmentally to our students; it is imperative that we gradually teach them the language skills needed to survive in the greater society. This is especially true for those teachers who view the language usage of inner-city children as appropriate for these children, instead of viewing it as critical to building a solid foundation for reading.

Another way to help students learn to use standard English is to provide and use reading materials that have immediate relevance to them. Pugh and Garcia (1990) maintained that literature plays a significant role in children's education about themselves and the world.

Teachers in urban settings need to know the literature of African-American, Hispanic, Native-American and Asian writers. They must make certain that this literature, which reflects the diversity of Americans, is a regular part of the curriculum, not just an added on or special interest section. Teachers and librarians need to examine the actual reading materials to which these children are exposed, in both the classroom and the school library. Children need to identify with both fictional and nonfictional works. Resources that will help teachers select materials include:

- *Hispanic American Classics and Best Loved Books for Children.* (Ada, 1987)
- *What Should Indian Students Read?* (Reyhner, 1988)
- *Black Authors and Illustrators of Children's Books.* (Rollock, 1988)
- *Eyeopeners! How to Choose and Use Children's Books About Real People, Places and Things.* (Korbrin, 1988)
- The Children's Choices, Young Adults' Choices and Teachers' Choices, of books published each fall in *The Reading Teacher* and *Journal of Reading.*

There are many resources available that help to promote reading enjoyment for urban children. Local storytellers, children's authors, and volunteer readers, as regular classroom contributors, are often overlooked resources in a community. Many of our children have been thrilled by St.

Louis children's author Patricia McKissack sharing her stories with them. Retired teachers, parents, and concerned citizens have also shared the joy of reading and storytelling with our children.

Teachers working with at-risk children must also be willing to expand their own knowledge and instructional techniques. When teaching at-risk children, it is not a question of should they have a skills-emphasis reading program or a whole language reading program—they will need both. These children need to spend each day practicing good reading habits. My own classes use a combination of whole language, direct instruction in phonics, oral reading, and listening comprehension. Each day the children spend an established time on independent reading, as well as time listening to me read to them.

As important as understanding language usage and identifying diverse materials are for urban teachers, there is also a need to recognize the importance of family life for at-risk children. Children have been labeled at risk because they come from low socioeconomic neighborhoods, dysfunctional families, or one-parent families. Many children entering school now were born to teenage parents and were drug addicted through birth or community contact. As a result, they react in one of two ways: They are withdrawn or are overly stimulated. The parents are unable to cope because of their own personal inadequacies and problems. These children need smaller classes where teachers can provide more individual attention.

The Tendency to Label Children

Labeling children because of their family or community background does very little to help them succeed in school. Most of these children are aware that they attend schools that are based on different, middle-class values and practices. Amuzie Chimezie (1988) pointed out several differences between the home environment and community of many children and the environment of the school. In the home community, children are free to engage in spontaneous behavior in speaking, in movement, and in emotional expression. However, in the school environment, children are expected to follow rules that require restraint in speech, in emotional expression, and in movement. As Perry Gilmore (1985) pointed out, students from lower income communities were rewarded for conducting themselves in what is regarded as acceptable (middle class) behavior and were punished for conducting themselves in what is regarded as unacceptable (lower class) behavior in schools. Anne McGill-Franzen and Richard Allington (1991) reminded us that every child has a right to literacy, and schools should not reward or punish children for the parents they have or the communities they come from. What these children need in order to succeed are teachers and school settings that promote their self-confidence, strengthen their background, and provide a secure educational environment.

To build self-confidence in urban children, teachers first need to believe these children can succeed in learning. The teachers must be able to communicate their expectations to the children and must be consistent in their classroom practices. For many children, their teacher serves as the "significant other" in their lives. Teachers serve as role models, cheerleaders, and counselors, as well as educators. The ability to show students that he or she cares for them and their futures is a critical factor for a teacher.

Some Important Factors

As a teacher, it is important to listen to each child, to establish standards for classroom behavior, to push each child to succeed, and to require that each child contribute daily to learning activities. Too often, at-risk children have been excused from making contributions to their own learning. The nonverbal behavior of a teacher affects many children who are at risk. When the body language of a teacher signals rejection and disapproval, children know it. They are very adept at reading their environment. A smile, a hug, or a nod of approval from a teacher can make the difference.

Hale-Benson (1988) contended that many urban African-American children lose their enthusiasm and excitement for school in the early primary grades because their creativity and freedom were blocked. According to Reitzammer (1990) and Sklarz (1989), the critical grade for children is the third grade. If at-risk children are not reached by this time, they are lost. One activity I have used successfully with urban children is a Friday afternoon program in which each child in my class is asked to share with classmates a poem, a reading, an oral interpretation, or an impromptu speech. This activity helped to build the confidence of children who were never required to share their ideas with others.

Another successful program has been a series of field trips, which enrich their lives and build background knowledge. However, it is not enough to take children on a field trip to visit a museum or to hear a symphony. They must be prepared for the experience. Before my children make a visit, they read about the event or the place. They are taught what behavior is required, so they know what is expected. Parents are encouraged to make these visits with their children so they can share the experience. After each field trip, there is always a discussion of what they saw, heard, or felt. This discussion is followed by a written assignment, which proved to be one of the most effective ways to broaden the cultural experiences of at-risk learners.

One significant factor has always been to include parents and guardians in the education of urban children. These family members care about their children, even if they do not exhibit this care in the same manner as those from middle-class environments. They need clearly stated strategies from teachers that will help them help their children succeed. This need is especially true for teenage parents. They need to know the importance of preparing their children for school and the importance for succeeding in school. Activities may include: (a) having the child(ren) regularly read to family members and be read to by family members; (b) encouraging family members to establish a regular time for completing homework; (c) having family members work with the child, at school, on a learning task; and (d) allowing family members to help supervise field trips.

The most effective way for educators to enlist the support of family members is through personal contact. We have learned that written correspondence sent to parents about reading programs will not have the same impact as face-to-face conversations. Many conversations will not take place in traditional school settings, but in community centers, social agencies, and religious institutions where family members can interact in a nonthreatening manner with school representatives. One of the most successful activities for urban parents has been a program that included both breakfast and luncheon meetings at school. Parents want to be involved in their children's learning; what they need from educators are realistic ways to help their children succeed.

An agenda for improving reading for at-risk students requires more than parents and teachers. As a practitioner who believes we can improve the reading experiences for at-risk urban children, I submit the following recommendations for teacher education programs, publishing companies, and schools:

Teacher Education Programs Need to Prepare Teachers to Work with Children in Urban Settings.   Student preservice teachers need to have early experiences in urban schools. They need to observe and work with these children as part of their educational training. New teachers assigned to work in schools in neighborhoods and communities in which they do not live do not understand the positive aspects of these communities and schools. Early exposure helps preservice teachers understand the differences in values and lifestyles.

Successful urban teachers should visit and share their experiences with preservice teachers.

Publishing Companies Should Make an Effort to Understand the Urban School Market.   They make a substantial profit from the sales of their teaching materials. A realistic look at their teaching materials will reveal that many do not truly represent the diversity of cultures in this country.

Publishing companies should use editors, authors, and artists that will present a factual representation of urban people and their culture. Not all urban children live in the ghetto or in a vacuum. Barry Herman (1977) proposed that we think positively when speaking of urban children, because of the variety of experiences and places that are possible for them such as trips to museums, libraries, theaters, civic centers, and zoos. He reminded us that the city world can be a thrilling and enriching place for children. Some urban children have two-parent families, attend movies, take trips, and visit places of interest in their cities. My own family lived in the inner city, and our son traveled abroad, visited museums, and enjoyed the theater, along with our neighbors' children. We must be careful as teachers not to label all children as deprived or disadvantaged because of the family's zip code. Many teachers have self-fulfilling prophecies in which everything about these children is underprivileged or lacking.

Teaching materials and activities that fit the mainstream of urban lifestyles must be prepared. My most successful activities involved hands-on activities, cooperative learning activities, small group activities, field trips, sharing stories, and playing games.

Because many inner-city children have experiences such as playing in the streets and running with groups of children (gangs), they cannot relate to the cultural experiences outlined in books used in many classrooms. It is difficult for many of these children to relate to stories that have the father going to the office to work, or children playing in the leaves with a pet dog or cat, or even the mother at home preparing and serving dinner. Pictures and stories in books and the classroom must not only mirror the lives of these children, but also offer realistic possibilities for improved lifestyles within their own communities. Teachers must talk with and share materials that inform these children about drug problems, personal health care, AIDS, political elections, war and conflict resolutions, bond issues for school improvements, teen parenting, and personal safety.

Teaching materials and learning activities must be used to help many inner-city students realize that staying in school is important. The message must be given that completing school does improve one's life; this is not just hypocrisy or a myth.

Schools Must Reexamine Their Commitment to Improving the Reading Abilities of At-Risk Urban Children.   One of the first recommendations for school representatives would be to meet with parents of at-risk children to let them know their children's academic potential. Parents must know their children's learning strengths as well as weaknesses. Also:

1. The curriculum must accurately provide what these children need in their educational preparation.

2. Schools also must promote cultural diversity throughout the school year and not just provide recognition of different races during one month of the year such as the common practice of having Black History Awareness in February.

3. Teachers must return to teaching in units where reading, writing, thinking, listening, and speaking are emphasized every day.

4. Instructional practices in schools must be reevaluated. One typical practice that needs to be examined is the "pull-out" model. This practice requires that problem readers be pulled out from the main classroom for small group instruction. Many times there is little communication between the pull-out teacher and the regular classroom teacher, so the child receives fragmented instruction. In addition, being pulled out of the regular classroom for remedial reading may stigmatize the pull-out

children. Teachers must be given time to coordinate their instructional planning for these students while schools investigate alternative methods of providing remediation.

5. Students in kindergarten through the third grade should devote a good bit of time to oral language development. Teachers should read aloud to students. Many teachers are so skill-oriented they feel they are wasting time if they are not teaching reading skills. Oral reading is an excellent way to strengthen reading skills and also foster the love of reading.

The Consistent Problem of an Inordinate Number of Boys Failing in Reading Development is Another Critical Area for Examination. T h e r e are usually more boys than girls in remedial reading classes. Research should investigate why boys typically need extra assistance in reading. The results would provide remedies for correction that classroom teachers could use.

TEACHERS ARE THE CORE OF THE EDUCATIONAL PROGRAM IN THIS COUNTRY

They must be challenged to teach and be rewarded for their results. As I talk to teachers, they relate their frustrations with the myriad of nonteaching responsibilities that take precious time away from teaching and learning. They must be relieved of nonteaching duties such as collecting and counting milk and lunch money, making redundant lists and reports, counting books and equipment, monitoring lunch and yard duties, and attending staff development meetings that have no significance for improving teaching or real usefulness in the classroom. There are too many programs that detract from the teaching/learning process. An especially distracting one is the fund raising that teachers and students must do in order to purchase school materials.

Teachers who work with at-risk children must realize that they serve as role models for these children. Children look up to their teachers and usually imitate their speech, dress, and attitude. Teachers must also appreciate the differences in these children and the values they bring to school. Each child is an individual and has had different experiences. Teachers need to be careful not to lump all children together in one category. The teacher must accept each child as he or she is and work lovingly to expose the child to acceptable behavior and values expected in the greater society. Teachers can do this by establishing simple rules of conduct for the classroom, which include good manners, positive expectations, and academic achievement.

One major problem that I have observed is that many schools do not strive for quality. Many teachers of at-risk students are not challenged to work toward excellence for these students. They are focused primarily on getting high test scores and controlled discipline.

It is demoralizing that many teachers are still concentrating on just teaching at-risk students the basic skills and maintaining discipline. One example of this was painfully clear to me during a recent visit to an elementary school. I was invited to participate in an internal evaluation at this school (K-5th grades), which had a substantial number of at-risk children enrolled. During an interview with a teacher, she spoke of how wonderful the students were because they did not cause discipline problems. So I asked her what were her goals for these children. She responded that she would teach them basic skills and how to behave as good citizens. She gave no indication that these children should strive for challenging learning activities, critical thinking activities, or for exposure to enriching learning experiences. She became annoyed when I asked her why did she not plan quest or enrichment type activities commonly used with children who are not labeled at-risk. At this point she terminated the interview.

We educators need to get away from the mindset that ethnically diverse, inner-city, or at-risk children need only to work on basic skills and appropriate classroom behavior. Enrichment and challenge should be a part of every child's learning. The best ways I have found to expand my students' learning included: (a) cooperative learning activities, thematic units that incorporate music and art with the other content areas and language arts subjects; and (b) grouping activities in which every child contributes to the learning. When teachers establish appropriate learning goals, use creative techniques, and establish a stable learning environment, our at-risk children excel in their learning. It is, indeed, sad that we educators continue to focus on the negatives with our at-risk students, instead of creating learning environments that promote excellence in education.

In teaching at-risk, urban children, teachers must be aware of the issues in the local school community, as well as state and global events that affect children. Personal safety, financial security, and individual rights and responsibilities all must be taught to these children. It is important to teach children about their world; as McCall, Higgins, and Karrels (1991) contended, teachers can actually increase their students' understanding of communities and foster the development of students who care about themselves and others. They must be readers themselves and translate information into the child's frame of reference.

Teachers must teach children just beginning school to listen and interact. Children must be encouraged to talk about what they are hearing and feeling as stories are shared.

Teachers must recognize how sensitive some children are to reading orally in front of their classmates. In my own classroom, oral reading is encouraged only after a child is prepared and expresses a desire to read.

Technology in the form of television, video games, and computerized toys have impacted reading. How can this fascination with technology be utilized in successful reading instruction?

When working with older readers, teachers must be able to identify the students' learning styles. Each person learns best by one or two methods, the most common being auditory and visual. Teachers need to pay attention to the modality used by their students. Busy work is an insult and boring to most children; they need to be challenged as well as supported in the most effective learning environment. Teaching to students' strengths rather than their weaknesses is one method that I have found successful. Also, to help students improve their learning, it is important for them to see themselves as problem solvers. These children need to predict and sample what they read. They must be given practice on using literal as well as inferential skills. Many children learn best when they work in teams or in small groups on reading projects. One major concern of the reading teacher is having students who are passive learners, as opposed to being active readers and learners. An instructional activity that worked to eliminate passivity has been to present children with a challenge word each day. This is a word that had to be defined and added to the student's vocabulary. At-risk children need to have a sense of accomplishment at the end of each day. The aforementioned activity fulfills this need.

Because many at-risk urban children have unique home lives, it helps when the teacher can serve as a sounding board, but not delve into the personal life of the child. The at-risk urban child does need tender, loving care, as well as a supportive and effective academic environment.

SUMMARY

I have been a classroom teacher, reading specialist, and administrator for the past 37 years in a large, urban school district. During this time many changes occurred in teaching strategies, in teacher preparation, and in students' willingness to accept what is being taught.

The Problem

Most inner-city children are considered at risk and are disproportionately represented in special education classes, school dropout statistics, low-level academic tracking programs, remedial reading classes, and inadequately financed schools.

Inner-city children can succeed in reading if given the same educational opportunities that children who are not at-risk are offered on a daily basis.

To become effective readers, students must be permitted and encouraged to use books and be given many opportunities to read. There is an abundance of available research findings on teaching methods, strategies, materials, effective schools, effective teachers, ethnic groups, and appropriate curriculum. Even though we have this research data, we are still producing mass numbers of inadequate readers. Now, it is time to implement the research recommendations and evaluate the results.

Four reasons often listed for low reading achievement are: (a) language usage; (b) family instability; (c) poor experiential background; and (d) differences between family values and school practices. These reasons must be analyzed, and incorrect assumptions about them dispelled in order for real achievement to take place.

Solutions

Teachers must understand that dialect is different, not deficient. The ultimate meaning is the same just stated differently. The children are intelligent and do understand standard English. The teacher must learn to adjust her own understanding of their dialect in order to teach them standard English. This can be accomplished through language experience stories for younger readers and portfolio writing for older readers. Students also must be encouraged to share in the use of oral language through storytelling and listening as others speak. The children's reading material must have some relevance in their lives.

Instability of family life, and teenage and/or ill-equipped parents are very real problems for many urban children. In fact, many of these children are homeless, live in foster homes, or have parents who abuse drugs. Parents and guardians must be included in the education of urban children. This can be achieved by including parents as supervisors on field trips, as room mothers/fathers, and as tutors at the school site.

The most effective way of reaching parents is through personal contact. Having breakfast or luncheon meetings are very effective ways to open lines of communication between the parents and the school. Parents want to be involved in their children's learning. However, many parents are at a loss as to how to approach the schools.

Field trips, where the children have been given in-depth preparation before the activity, prove to be one of the most effective ways for broadening the cultural experiences of at-risk learners. These experiences provide opportunities for listening, observing, reading, writing, critical thinking, and speaking.

There should be collaboration between preservice teachers and successful experienced teachers. This would provide positive role models for beginning teachers. It is also important that teachers learn of the positive aspect of communities in which they work, but do not live.

Schools must recommit their efforts in providing appropriate and challenging curriculum and utilizing dedicated, well-trained, sensitive teachers to ensure successful learning. Teachers must be relieved of the numerous nonteaching duties and added-on programs. Classes must be smaller so that children can receive more individual attention.

We, as educators, must rid ourselves of the mindset that inner-city children are to be taught only basics. Instead, we must begin to focus on their strengths in order to overcome their weaknesses.

REFERENCES

Ada, A. (1987). Hispanic American classics and best loved books for children. *Journal of Reading, 31*, 195–202.

Cecil, N. (1988). Black dialect and academic success: A study of teacher expectations. *Reading Improvement, 25*(1), 34–38.

Chimezie, A. (1988). Black children's characteristics and the school: A selective adaptation approach. *The Western Journal of Black Studies, 12*(2), 77–85.

Christensen, L. (1990). Teaching standard English: Whose standard? *English Journal, 79*(2), 36–40.

Dummett, L. (1984). The enigma—the persistent failure of black children in learning to read. *Reading World, 24*(1), 31–37.

Gilmore, P. (1985). "Gimme room:" School resistance, attitude, and access to literacy. *Journal of Education, 167*(1), 111–128.

Hale-Benson, J. (1988). *Black children, their roots, culture, and learning styles* (3rd ed.). Baltimore: The John Hopkins University Press.

Korbrin, B. (1988). *Eyeopeners! How to choose and use children's books about real people, places and things.* New York: Penguin.

McCall, A., Higgins, J., & Karrels, A. (1991). Infusing a community unit with the concept of caring. *Social Studies and the Young Learner, 4*(2), 13–15.

McGill-Franzen, A., & Allington, R. (1991). Every child's right: Literacy. *The Reading Teacher, 45*(2), 86–89.

O'Bruba, W. (1986). The black child, his dialect, and his reading. *Reading Horizons, 26*(3), 185–188.

Pugh, S., & Garcia, J. (1990). Portraits in black: Establishing African American identity through nonfiction books. *Journal of Reading, 34*(1), 20–25.

Reitzammer, A. (1990). Reading success: A cornerstone of dropout prevention, *Reading Improvement, 24*(4), 287–288.

Reyhner, J. (1988). What should indian students read. In J. Reyhner (Ed.), *Teaching the Indian child: A bilingual/multicultural approach* (2nd Ed., pp. 142–161). Billings, MT: Eastern Montana College.

Rollock, B. (1988). *Black authors and illustrators of children's books* (Vol. 660). New York: Garland Reference Library.

Sklarz, D. (1989). Keep at-risk students in school by keeping them up to grade level. *The American School Board Journal, 176*(9), 33–34.

7

Understanding Agenda Setting in Reading Research

Peter B. Mosenthal
Syracuse University

Recently, much discussion and debate in reading (e.g., Edelsky, 1990; McKenna, Robinson, & Miller, 1990) and education (e.g., Glass, 1987; Finn, 1988) framed inquiry in research in terms of the metaphor of agenda setting. Implicit in this metaphor are the assumptions that agendas are set to achieve a goal or solve a problem and that agendas consist of a list of prescribed actions which, when followed, ideally will accomplish the chosen goal or solve the selected problem.

Although these assumptions appear to be neutral, they actually entail four important socio-political questions: (a) What goals should be viewed as ideal and what problems should be identified as most pressing in setting an agenda? (b) What are the most effective procedures for carrying out the prescribed actions of an agenda? (c) Who should have the authority to set agendas? and (d) Who should benefit from agendas once they have been carried out?

Obviously these questions are not independent. As Glass (1987) and Schön (1987) reminded us, how questions (a), (b), and (d) are answered often depends on how question (c) is determined. Because different researchers perceive the goals and problems of reading and education differently, they tend to set research agendas in these areas differently. Moreover, because researchers often perceive goals and problems as occurring at different levels in a bureaucratic hierarchy (e.g., reading group, classroom, school, school district, county, state, or national level), they tend to set agendas that differentially benefit individuals and groups representative of these different levels. Finally, because different researchers subscribe to different and often competing methodologies (Mosenthal & Kamil, 1991;

Popkewitz, 1984), they often view these methodologies as being the most effective procedures for defining and carrying out prescribed actions of an agenda.

In addressing these four questions, researchers have viewed the problem of agenda setting in reading idiosyncratically: Researchers compete to become the recognized authority in the area of reading research; those so recognized are given license to present their particular reading research agenda for public consideration. Given this authority and a public forum, researchers begin by identifying their favorite reading goals or problems (locally or globally defined). Based on researchers' favorite methodology for observing, categorizing, and analyzing data, prescribed procedures that carry out the actions of a reading research agenda are defined and implemented. Finally, depending on researchers' selected sample, certain individuals and groups may benefit whereas others may be placed at a distinct disadvantage as an agenda's actions are implemented (Shannon, 1991).

When viewed collectively, researchers' seemingly idiosyncratic approaches to conducting reading research have traditionally represented a center-to-periphery approach to agenda setting (Mosenthal & Kamil, 1991; Popkewitz, 1984). In the following section, this approach is briefly described. This approach is then considered in light of three very different perspectives of what the problems and goals of reading are and should be, respectively. The implication of these perspectives for setting a collective reading research agenda are considered. The chapter concludes by arguing that the principal problem with reading research is that researchers have ignored the problem of goal and problem setting as an important first step toward setting a collective reading research agenda.

THE CENTER-TO-PERIPHERY APPROACH
TO AGENDA SETTING

Until recently, the dominant approach to agenda setting in reading research was the center-to-periphery approach (Mosenthal & Kamil, 1991; Popkewitz, 1984). Underlying this approach is the belief that change is always for the "better." Better, in turn, is viewed in terms of the following chain of reasoning (Mosenthal, 1985): Because reading research created it, it is therefore new; because it is new, it is therefore improved; and because it is improved, let us adopt it!

To set such center-to-periphery thinking into practice, reading researchers used the following set of agenda-setting procedures. They begin by identifying their favorite problem or goal, which is usually associated with only one or two of the six contexts that make up any reading situation (Mosenthal, 1984b; Mosenthal & Kamil, 1991). Problems may be inherent in the readers (e.g., lack of prior knowledge, motivation, or metacognitive ability); they may arise because of input constraints in the materials (e.g., difficult vocabulary, complicated syntax, or inappropriate typographic format; the problems may be related to inappropriate administration procedure characteristics (e.g., questions that require a "level of processing" beyond the reader's ability, instructions that may be too numerous to follow).

The reading problems may have to do with the scoring procedures and scoring criteria used in a study (e.g., cut scores are set too low or too high; number of qualitative categories are too numerous); they may be associated with the *situation organizer* (e.g., the teacher teaches based on overly low expectations for a group of readers); or they may involve factors related to *setting* (e.g., students are placed in a inappropriate reading group; the home environment does not encourage bedtime reading).

Again, reading problems may arise because of a combination of variables related to these contexts (e.g., the selection of a boring text for an uninterested student, by a teacher who has low expectations for this student, who was unwisely placed in a low-level reading group in an inner-city school with few printed materials).

Goals, on the other hand, may involve overcoming problems associated with a given context (e.g., improving poor prior knowledge or metacognitive ability associated with the reader context), or simply may involve finding ways to improve readers' performance by optimizing contextual conditions (e.g., simplifying the vocabulary in the input materials, or encouraging reading groups to function collaboratively).

Once reading researchers have identified their favorite problem or goal, they then validate this problem or goal by using a basic experimental paradigm (e.g., showing that good readers have more of some ability or are able to make use of more of some strategy than do poor readers; demonstrating that students using one method read better than students using another method; or verifying that one set of input conditions optimize readers' output more than another set of input conditions) (Mosenthal, 1988b).

Following the validation phase of their studies, reading researchers next disseminate and market their findings. In this stage, efforts are made to convince practitioners that their problems and goals are similar (if not identical) to the problems and goals already investigated by reading researchers.

If this dissemination and marketing phase is successful, reading researchers enter a development phase where they devise a set of materials (or even an entire program) that is consistent with the solution identified in their experiment. In the dissemination phase, reading researchers market their materials and program to further convince practitioners that their current instructional agendas need to be modified to incorporate the "latest discoveries in research."

In the final adoption/installation phase, reading practitioners proceed by modifying their reading instructional agendas to accommodate the new research innovation. In so doing, practitioners replaced their agenda items with those of reading researchers (Mosenthal, 1986).

Although this center-to-periphery approach has traditionally been the most pervasive approach to setting agendas in reading research, it is certainly not without its limitations. To understand these limitations, consider this approach in light of questions (a), (c), and (d) addressed earlier, beginning with question (a) (i.e., What are the basic problems and ideal goals that direct the setting of agendas in reading research?). More often than not, in the center-to-periphery approach, problems and goals tend to be locally defined. Moreover, they tend to be motivated by theoretical concerns that have little, if anything, to do with the problems of practitioners (Kamil, 1984; Mosenthal, 1984a, 1986; Popkewitz, 1984; Schön, 1987). Being locally defined, there are as many operationally defined problems and goals as there are individual reading researchers.

Even to the extent to which idiosyncratic problems and goals may be classified as "lines of research" (Mosenthal & Kamil, 1991), those many lines present a myriad of equally valid choices. Because each study and line of reading research is replete with its own internal validity, there is no basis for choosing the problem and goal of one study (or one line of research) over another. Concomitantly, without more globally specified problems and goals, there is no way to determine when an outcome of a study represents a significant change for the better (i.e., when an outcome represents an "improvement"), or merely represents a change for the sake of change (Mosenthal, 1987, 1989). Further, without being able to determine whether one outcome is better than another, there is no basis to determine which actions should be placed on an agenda (either a researcher's research agenda or a practitioner's instructional agenda) and which actions are better left off.

In summary, given the current state of affairs, agenda setting in reading research is carried out in the context of local problems and goals. The primary focus of this research is on the theoretical means for solving these problems and achieving these goals. Without globally defined problems and goals, there is no basis to determine which local problems and goals are better. And not knowing which goals are evaluatively better, there is no basis for deciding which means are better. Therefore, agenda setting in reading research is largely irrational and nondeterministic (Mosenthal, 1985, 1987).

The second limitation to agenda setting is related to the question: Who has the legitimacy to set agendas in reading research? Characteristic of the center-to-periphery approach to agenda setting, it is usually researchers, as experts, who set the reading research agenda, which gets translated into the instructional agenda (Popkewitz, 1984; Schön, 1987). The specious assumption here is that the problems and goals of researchers are assumed to be the same as those of practitioners and other client groups (e.g., students, parents, and bureaucrats), whose problems researchers are supposedly solving and whose goals researchers are supposedly facilitating (Kelly, 1980; Mosenthal, 1984a, 1986). Yet, often researchers' theoretically defined problems and goals have little to do with the problems and goals of practitioners and clients (Popkewitz, 1984; Schön, 1987). By excluding practitioners and clients as legitimate contributors to the reading research agenda, reading researchers fail to identify the "real" (or "relevant") problems and goals of practitioners and clients—not only at a global level but also at a local level. Although this may be interpreted as an issue of power (e.g., Cochran-Smith & Lytle, 1990), it is also an issue of providing relevant and much more useful services to practitioners and clients who need and seek these services (Kelly, 1980; Mosenthal, 1984a).

In short, by failing to include practitioners and clients in setting their research agendas, reading researchers have ignored the real problems and goals that they are purportedly entrusted to solve and facilitate. Even to the extent that local and diverse practitioner and client problems may bear resemblance to the local and diverse problems identified in research, reading researchers have not developed a systematic dissemination system to match the two. Rather, the assumption is maintained that reading researchers as experts know best: "Our problems and goals are your problems and goals; thus, reading practitioners and clients need not be listed among those who set reading research agendas."

The third limitation to agenda setting in reading research is related to the question, "Who benefits once reading research agendas have been set and carried out?" As suggested earlier, because the problems and goals that are identified in the agendas of reading researchers are not usually the same problems and goals of practitioners and clients, practitioners and clients seldom directly benefit from the actions taken in carrying out reading researchers' agendas (Schön, 1979, 1987). However, equally problematic is the issue that, even if reading researchers did consider practitioners and client groups, which practitioners and client groups in particular should benefit?

Education serves an extremely diverse group of practitioners and clients in the United States, including bureaucrats at local, state, and national levels; school administrators, teachers, instructional designers, and curriculum coordinators; diverse racial, ethnic, and gender groups; advantaged and disadvantaged populations; parents and children; and at-risk and gifted children. To date, whereas different reading researchers (e.g., Edelsky, 1990; Fraatz, 1987; Wallace & Walberg, 1991) champion different benefactors in particular, little debate has focused on why it is more important that one group be served in setting a research agenda than another. As Kelly (1980) suggested, this decision could not be made without having first identified what constitutes significant global problems.

In brief, the assumption that "one size fits all" (Mosenthal, 1984b) or "one reading research agenda benefits all practitioners and clients" is hardly tenable. Given limited research and implementation resources, the issue that needs to be addressed by reading researchers is, "Whose problems and goals should be addressed in reading research?" and "Why should the problems and goals of this group be addressed and not those of some other group?" Again, until these questions are answered, reading research, as a means for promoting progress, will represent random activity without direction (Mosenthal, 1985).

To provide a basis for answering these questions, the following section identifies three principal perspectives that implicitly frame the problems and goals of reading research.

THREE PERSPECTIVES BY WHICH THE PROBLEMS AND GOALS OF READING RESEARCH AGENDAS ARE FRAMED

Although there are perhaps as many problems and goals in reading as there are reading researchers and practitioners, these problems and goals broadly reflect three general perspectives: the administrative efficiency, the client-satisfaction, and the emancipatory perspective. Consider these three perspectives as possible starting points for understanding the problems and goals that should be included in reading research agendas.

The Administrative-Efficiency Perspective

As viewed by supporters of the administrative-efficiency perspective, one goal of education (and reading) should be to socialize new generations in the cultural, social, intellectual, and moral values of previous generations (e.g., Bloom, 1987; Hirsch, 1987). A second goal should be to ensure that the broad range of job demands are met so that the viability of our nation's economy is maintained (Mincer, 1989; National Center on Education and the Economy, 1990; U. S. Departments of Labor and Education, 1988). Associated with these goals is the problem of how to socialize students and meet the human resource needs of society but minimize administrative costs (House, 1991; Kelly, 1980).

To accomplish these goals and solve this problem, proponents of the administrative-efficiency perspective have argued the need for "top-down" decision making, with standards defined at global levels (e.g., national and state levels) and implemented at local levels (e.g., county and school district level) (Darling-Hammond & Wise, 1985). Standards are further ensured and costs minimized through the use of commercially prepared instructional materials, standardized and competency-based tests, and national assessments. To address discrepancies between human resource needs and worker abilities, proponents of this perspective further argue there is the need to extend the number of years of required schooling and/or to realign school curricula to make it more consistent with workplace demands (Johnston & Packer, 1987; Resnick, 1987).

Researchers (e.g., McKenna, Robinson, & Miller, 1990) who have implicitly endorsed the "academic approach" within the administrative efficiency perspective have viewed the goal of reading as promoting a common language and literacy culture, so there can be mutual communication among all members of society (Walmsley, 1981). This, in part, is made possible largely so all readers will learn to respond and interpret text in a standardized manner consistent with the criteria set forth by some authority of society, such as politicians, bureaucrats, researchers, teachers, or test designers (Fish, 1980; Olson, 1977).

Concomitant with this goal, researchers have viewed the problem of reading as the problem of teaching students to extract meaning from text in the most cost-effective manner possible (Mosenthal, 1984a). This can be accomplished through the use of commercially published basal reader programs, standardized tests, and informal reading inventories (Chall & Squire, 1991). When translated into practice, the assumptions of the academic approach are reflected largely in terms of *discrete skills acquisition* whereby students are uniformly taught to decode linguistic information in a text, recode this information in memory relative to some ideal schema, and then reencode this information again, as is required by some question or directive issued by some situation organizer (Mosenthal, 1988a). Reader ability in this approach is largely defined in terms of students' performance on norm-referenced reading tests.

Researchers who have tacitly endorsed the "utilitarian approach" within the administrative-efficiency perspective have viewed the goal of reading as one of teaching readers to perform those tasks that define functional competence in a society and/or in a particular setting (e.g., the workplace) (Heath, 1980; Kirsch & Jungeblut, 1986; Scribner & Cole, 1981). This, in part, is made possible largely so all readers will learn to meet the minimum criteria that define functional competence for a set of tasks in an applied domain (Walmsley, 1981). Such criteria might include properly filling out an income tax form, signing one's name to a social security card on the appropriate line, or correctly interpreting a jury summons so that one knows what time to appear in court (Kirsch & Mosenthal, 1990).

Consistent with this goal, researchers have viewed the problem of reading as the problem of teaching students how to transfer performance from reading tasks in an instructional domain to reading tasks in an applied domain (Mikulecky & Drew, 1991), again, in the most client-effective manner possible. The principal means for accomplishing this is through the use of competency-based instructional programs whereby students are taught lists of specific tasks that comprise a specific domain. Reader ability, in this approach, is largely defined in terms of students' performance on minimum-competence tests.

In summary, under the administrative efficiency perspective, the goals and problems for setting an educational agenda, in general (and a reading research agenda, in particular), have been defined in terms of maximizing cultural homogenization, social functioning, and economic stability but minimizing (even reducing) costs (e.g., Hawley, 1990). To these ends, the persons who have legitimacy for setting these agendas tend to include high-level administrators and bureaucrats who set cultural, social, and economic standards. Goals and problems are then articulated in terms of these standards (e.g., Cross, 1990; Finn, 1988) which, in turn, become the higher level goals and problems of national and state educational agendas. These agendas are published as reports calling for "new" reforms (e.g., U. S. Department of Education, 1986). Reading researchers, whose individual goals and identified problems are consistent with these national agendas, are provided funding at nominal costs to further define and address these goals and problems in a center-to-periphery fashion. In this regard, the goals and problems of reading research agendas are defined reactively rather than proactively; reading research funding follows administratively defined reforms, and reading research then follows the funding (House, 1991).

When the question is asked, "Who benefits from this perspective of agenda setting?" the typical response is "The good of society is advanced for the benefit of the individual" (cf. Murray, 1984). The argument here is that raising expected standards for all citizens will increase actual performance standards. This, in turn, will lead to greater employment opportunities and higher standards of living for all citizens. Moreover, it will lead to a better educated work force, which, in turn, will increase worker productivity and, therefore, will make the United States more economically competitive. And the added benefit to these societal benefits is they can all be achieved at reduced costs!

The Client-Satisfaction Perspective

As viewed by supporters of the client-satisfaction perspective, the goal of education should be to address the goals and problems of all individuals, so that each individual can develop a sense of "autonomy," "self-worth," and "self-ownership" (Spring, 1975), and each individual can reach his or her maximum potential (Neill, 1960). Associated with these goals is the problem of defining the full range of individual differences that make up society and how best to address these differences, so the spectra of individual goals can be adequately addressed and the varieties of individual problems effectively solved, whatever the cost (Kelly, 1980; Mosenthal 1984a).

To accomplish these ends, proponents of the client-satisfaction perspective have argued the need for "bottom-up" decision making, with goals and problems defined and negotiated at local levels (Popkewitz, 1984). This is assumed to be accomplished, in part, by training teachers to be researchers. Being both practitioners and researchers at a local level, teachers can identify and implement their appropriate agenda so that individual students' goals can be identified and their individual problems solved (Cochran-Smith & Lytle, 1990).

Researchers (e.g., Edelsky, 1990; Goodman, 1989) who have tacitly endorsed the client-satisfaction perspective have viewed the goals of reading as valuing the following: differences among learners who come to school and differences in objectives and outcomes as they progress through school; expansion "on the learners' strengths and maximum growth, not conformity and uniformity"; and empowerment of learners, so that they "take ownership over their learning and (are) given maximum support in developing their own objectives and fulfilling them" (Goodman, 1989, p. 209).

Accompanying these goals is the problem, as viewed by researchers, of extending children's natural language abilities through the use of "authentic" speech acts and literacy events that use four modalities of language (i.e., reading writing, listening, and speaking). A related problem is teaching children how to set their own "learning agendas," and how to carry out these agendas, so their personal goals are achieved and their individual problems are solved (Short & Burke, 1989). The principal means for accomplishing these ends are through the use of whole language instructional programs, as well as the use of individualized remedial programs such as Reading Recovery (Pinnell, 1989). Evaluation, in this approach, ranges from the use of portfolio assessments to less formal but ongoing observation and analysis (Goodman, Goodman, & Hood, 1989; Roderick, 1991).

In summary, under the client-satisfaction perspective, the goals and problems for setting an educational agenda, in general (and a reading research agenda in particular), are defined largely by the clients that agendas are designed to serve. To these ends, the legitimate persons for setting these agendas are students and their teachers, who set agendas, so the range of classroom goals and problems are considered (if not addressed) in an ongoing fashion.

When the question is asked, "Who benefits from this perspective of agenda setting?" the typical response is, "The good of the individual is advanced for the benefit of society." The argument here is that raising individuals who have the wherewithal to set their own agendas, identify their own goals, and solve their own problems empowers them to pursue their own destinies and become model citizens, much like Thomas Jefferson envisioned, without relying on some higher authority to address these concerns (cf. Shannon, 1991).

The Emancipatory Perspective

As viewed by supporters of the emancipatory perspective (e.g., Friere, 1970; Giroux, 1989), the goal of education should be to change the educational, social, and political structure so the oppressed may forge a new, more egalitarian relation with their oppressors. According to emancipationists, this goal is necessary because of the problems raised by operating within an administrative-efficiency perspective and center-to-periphery approach to agenda setting. Because administrators, bureaucrats, and researchers set agendas that favor their own social class and status, there is discrimination against certain groups and classes of people (Bowles & Gintis, 1976; Merton, 1972). The problem of hegemonic goal identification and problem setting should be replaced with a much more egalitarian approach to agenda setting that is particularly sensitive to the needs of minority groups.

To accomplish these ends, proponents of the emancipatory perspective have called for the need to adopt a "critical theory approach" to emancipation (Habermas, 1972). Here, research must give rise to understanding that "elucidates and criticizes those features of the human situation that frustrate intentional agency" (Sullivan, 1984, p. 123). Furthermore, this approach should "inform and guide the activities of a class of dissatisfied actors—revealing how the irrationalities of social life which are causing the dissatisfaction can be eliminated by taking some specific action which the theory calls for" (Fay, 1975, p. 98).

Researchers (e.g., Friere, 1970; Giroux, 1989; Gordon, Miller, & Rollock, 1990) who openly endorse the emancipationist perspective have viewed the goal of reading as understanding "the linkages between the structural dynamics of (one's) class, race, and projects of human agents embedded in this historically constituted structures" and the consequent ability to transform these dynamics (Sullivan, 1984, p. 124). Accompanying this goal, researchers (e.g., Gordon et al., 1990) have viewed the problem of reading as social and political in nature. For one, most reading research studies focus on White readers; very few studies are designed to address the goals and problems of readers of minority classes. So, the goals and problems are all but neglected. Moreover, the researchers who identify goals and problems tend to be largely White, middle-class individuals; seldom, if ever, are reading researchers from minority groups or classes. As such, goals and problems, when formulated in research, tend to always reflect those attitudes and biases of the White, middle class. Finally, because teachers are also White, they tend to interpret the goals and problems of minority students in terms of their own cultural biases (Au & Mason, 1981).

These problems were particularly well expressed by Gordon et al. (1990) as they relate to African Americans:

> Examination of the social and educational research knowledge bases relative to Afro-Americans indicated that these sciences have traditionally attempted to understand the life experiences of Afro-Americans from a narrow cultrocentric perspective and against equally narrow cultrocentric standards. Diversity has been viewed as deviance and differences have been viewed as deficits. Thus, the issue of cultural and ethnic diversity has been incompletely or inadequately assessed, and has insufficiently influenced knowledge production. These problems are compounded when we recognize that the tradi-

tionally dominant, communicentric bias not only frames the conceptual paradigms we use to study social phenomena, but also frames many of the core
propositions upon which the sciences rest, such as objectivity, positivism, and
empiricism, which are cultural products and thus may be culture-bound.
These hallmarks of science may be more limited in their explanatory usefulness than is generally presumed. (p. 15)

In summary, under the emancipationist perspective, the goal for setting
an educational agenda, in general (and a reading research agenda particular), is to ensure that all classes of individuals have the power to place items
on these agendas, so their goals and problems are acknowledged and
addressed in a egalitarian manner. When the question is asked, "Who
benefits from this perspective of agenda setting?" the response from this
perspective is, "The good of all classes (and especially the minority classes)
are advanced for the benefit of society." The argument here is that, as a
society, we are committed to treating all people equally, regardless of race,
creed, and gender. Moreover, by recognizing and encouraging cultural
diversity, we, as a nation, will have not only a richer heritage but also the
ability to enlarge on "new possibilities born of a plurality of perspectives"
(cf. Sullivan, 1984).

SUMMARY AND CONCLUSIONS

The purposes of this chapter were to describe how agendas in reading
research tend to be set and to identify the perspectives that frame goal and
problem identification in the setting of reading research agendas. Implicit
in this discussion has been the argument that reading researchers, in setting
their agendas, tend to ignore the ends of agenda setting and focus largely
on the means. In this regard, they view the problem of agenda setting
largely as a "problem-solving" rather than as a "problem-setting" problem;
they view the goal of agenda setting largely as "the goal of goal attainment"
rather than as "the goal of goal identification" (Schön, 1979). Moreover, they
tend to define problems and goals locally, largely motivated by theoretical
concerns, rather than by actual situations. In adopting a center-to-periphery
approach, the common practice has been for reading researchers to make
practitioners and other clients believe that the problems and goals of
researchers are the problems and goals of practitioners/clients. Once this
has been accomplished, researchers then translate their "solution conditions" into a program that practitioners or clients can use to solve the
researchers' problems and accomplish researchers' goals.

It has been argued that reading research, when viewed in the broad
context of educational goals, is carried out by researchers from an administrative-efficiency perspective. This perspective stands in distinct contrast
with the client-satisfaction and the emancipationist perspectives. It has
been noted that associated with each of these perspectives is a significantly

different set of goals and problems, which, in turn, suggest very different ends of what should be included in a reading research agenda. Additionally, each perspective suggests different answers to the questions, "Who has the legitimacy to set agendas in reading research?" and "Who benefits once reading research agendas have been set and carried out?"

In short, as these three perspectives illustrate, there are a variety of ways that agendas can be set in reading research. Each has associated with it, its own ends and its own means and each has its own benefactors. The problem this poses for setting a reading research agenda includes the questions:

- Given these three perspectives, which of these should frame the way that goals are identified and problems are set in reading research?
- Why should the goals and problems of one perspective be chosen instead of others?
- Why should certain groups have the power to set reading research agendas and not others?
- Why should certain individuals and groups benefit from the setting and carrying out of a reading research agenda rather than others?

Whereas these questions may appear to be easily answered by those who maintain a strong bias for a given perspective (cf. Edelsky, 1990), it should be noted that the enterprise of reading research and instruction, like the enterprise of schooling, involves all these perspectives, at one level or another. As Cuban (1990) suggested, the real issue is not how to achieve the goals and solve the problems of education and reading from a single perspective at a single time; doing so only results in a pendulum of reform swinging back and forth between the administrative-efficiency perspective and the client-satisfaction perspective. It is, perhaps, not until a reading research agenda is set that incorporates the goals and problems of all three perspectives that real progress can be made. Determining how this can be accomplished should be the collective goal and problem of the entire reading community, including clients as well as researchers.

REFERENCES

Au, K. H., & Mason, J. M. (1981). Social organization factors in learning to read: The balance of rights hypothesis. *Reading Research Quarterly, 17*, 115–152.

Bloom, A. (1987). *The closing of the American mind.* New York: Simon & Schuster.

Bowles, S., & Gintis, H. (1976). *Schooling in capitalist America: Educational reform and the contradictions of economic life.* New York: Basic Books.

Chall, J. S., & Squire, J. R. (1991). The publishing industry and textbooks. In R. Barr, M. L. Kamil, P. B. Mosenthal, & P. D. Pearson (Eds.), *Handbook of reading research* (Vol. 2, pp. 120–146). New York: Longman.

Cochran-Smith, M., & Lytle, S. L. (1990). Research on teaching and teacher research: The issues that divide. *Educational Researcher, 19*, 2–11.

Cross, C. T. (1990). National goals: Four priorities for educational researchers. *Educational*

Researcher, 19, 21–24.

Cuban, L. (1990). Reforming again, again, and again. *Educational Researcher, 19,* 3–13.

Darling-Hammond, L., & Wise, A. E. (1985). Beyond standardization: State standards and school improvement. *Elementary School Journal, 85,* 315–336.

Edelsky, C. (1990). Whose agenda is this anyway? A response to McKenna, Robinson, and Miller. *Educational Researcher, 19,* 7–11.

Fay, B. (1975). *Social theory and political practice.* New York: G. Allen.

Finn, C. E., Jr. (1988). What ails education research. *Educational Researcher, 17,* 5–8.

Fish, S. (1980). *Is there a text in this class? The authority of interpretative communities.* Cambridge, MA: Harvard University Press.

Fraatz, J. M. B. (1987). *The politics of reading: Power, opportunities, and the prospects of change in America's public schools.* New York: Teachers College Press.

Friere, P. (1970). *Pedagogy of the oppressed.* New York: Seabury.

Giroux, H. (1989). *Schooling and the struggle for public life: Critical pedagogy in the modern age.* Minneapolis, MN: University of Minnesota Press.

Glass, G. V. (1987). What works: Politics and research. *Educational Researcher, 16,* 5–10.

Goodman, K. S. (1989). Whole-language research: Foundations and development. *Elementary School Journal, 90,* 207–221.

Goodman, K. S., Goodman, Y. M., & Hood, W. J. (Eds.) (1989). *The whole language evaluation book.* Portsmouth, NH: Heinemann.

Gordon, E. W., Miller, F., & Rollock, D. (1990). Coping with communicentric bias in knowledge production in the social sciences. *Educational Researcher, 19,* 14–19.

Habermas, J. (1972). *Knowledge and human interest.* Boston: Beacon Press.

Hawley, W. D. (1990). Enhancing the Federal Government's capacity to support the improvement of education through research and development. *Educational Researcher, 19,* 17–22.

Heath, S. B. (1980). The functions and uses of literacy. *Journal of Communication, 30,* 123–133.

Hirsch, E. D., Jr. (1987). *Cultural literacy: What every American needs to know.* Boston: Houghton Mifflin.

House, E. R. (1991). Big policy, little policy. *Educational Researcher, 20,* 21–26.

Johnston, W. B., & Packer, A. H. (1987). *Workforce 2000: Work and workers for the 21st century.* Indianapolis, IN: Hudson Institute.

Kamil, M. (1984). Current traditions of reading research. In P. D. Pearson, R. Barr, M. L. Kamil, & P. B. Mosenthal (Eds.), *Handbook of reading research* (Vol. 1, pp. 39–62). New York: Longman.

Kelly, R. M. (1980). Ideology, effectiveness, and public sector productivity: With illustrations form the field of higher education. *Journal of Social Issues, 36,* 76–95.

Kirsch, I. S., & Jungeblut, A. (1986). *Literacy: Profiles of America's young adults (Final Report)* (NAEP Report No. 16-PL-01). Princeton, NJ: Educational Testing Service.

Kirsch, I. S., & Mosenthal, P. B. (1990). Exploring document literacy: Variables underlying the performance of young adults. *Reading Research Quarterly, 25,* 5–30.

McKenna, M. C., Robinson, R. D., & Miller, J. W. (1990). Whole language: A research agenda for the nineties. *Educational Researcher, 19,* 3–6.

Merton, R. K. (1972). Insiders and outsiders: A chapter in the sociology of knowledge. In H.S. Becker (Ed.), *Varieties of political expression in sociology* (pp. 9–47). Chicago, IL: University of Chicago Press.

Mikulecky, L., & Drew, R. (1991). Basic literacy skills in the workplace. In R. Barr, M. L. Kamil, P. B. Mosenthal, & P. D. Pearson (Eds.), *Handbook of reading research* (Vol. 2, pp. 669–689). New York: Longman.

Mincer, J. (1989). Human capital and the labor market: A review of current research. *Educational Researcher, 18,* 27–34.

Mosenthal, P. B. (1984a). Defining reading program effectiveness: An ideological perspective. *Poetics, 13,* 195–216.

Mosenthal, P. B. (1984b). The problem of partial specification in translating reading research into practice. *Elementary School Journal, 85,* 199–227.

Mosenthal, P. B. (1985). Defining progress in educational research. *Educational Researcher, 14,* 3–9.

Mosenthal, P. B. (1986). Improving reading practice with reading theory. The Procrustean approach. *Reading Teacher, 40,* 108–111.

Mosenthal, P. B. (1987). Rational and irrational approaches to understanding reading. *Reading Teacher, 40,* 570–572.

Mosenthal, P. B. (1988a). Meaning in the storage-and-conduit metaphor of reading. *Reading Teacher, 41,* 582–584.

Mosenthal, P. B. (1988b). The simplicity approach to solving reading research puzzles. *Reading Teacher, 41,* 818–821.

Mosenthal, P. B. (1989). Defining problems in reading research. *Reading Teacher, 42,* 718–719.

Mosenthal, P. B., & Kamil, M. L. (1991). Understanding progress in reading research. In P. B. Mosenthal, M. L. Kamil, & P. D. Pearson (Eds.), *Handbook of reading research* (Vol. 2, pp. 1013–1046). New York: Longman.

Murray, C. (1984). *Losing ground: American social policy, 1950–1980.* New York: Basic Books.

National Center on Education and the Economy. (1990, June). *America's choice: High skills or low wages* (The report of the Commission on the Skills of the American Workforce). Rochester, NY: Author.

Neill, A. S. (1960). *Summerhill.* New York: Hart.

Olson, D. R. (1977). From utterance to text: The bias of language in speech and writing. *Harvard Educational Review, 47,* 257–281.

Pinnell, G. S. (1989). Reading recovery: Helping at-risk children learn to read. *Elementary School Journal, 90,* 161–183.

Popkewitz, T. (1984). *Paradigm and ideology in educational research: The social functions of the intellectual.* New York: Falmer Press.

Resnick, L. B. (1987). Learning in school and out. *Educational Researcher, 16,* 13–20.

Roderick, J. A. (Ed.). (1991). *Context-responsive approaches to assessing children's language.* Urbana, IL: National Conference on Research in English.

Schön, D. A. (1979). Generative metaphor: A perspective on problem-setting in social policy. In A. Ortony (Ed.), *Metaphor and thought* (pp. 254–283). Cambridge, England: Cambridge University Press.

Schön, D. A. (1987). *Educating the reflective practitioner.* San Francisco: Jossey-Bass.

Scribner, S., & Cole, M. (1981). *The psychology of literacy.* Cambridge, MA: Harvard University Press.

Shannon, P. (1991). Politics, policy, and reading research. In R. Barr, M. L. Kamil, P. B. Mosenthal, & P. D. Pearson (Eds.), *Handbook of reading research* (Vol. 2, pp. 147–167). New York: Longman.

Short, K. G., & Burke, C. L. (1989). New potentials for teacher education: Teaching and learning as inquiry. *Elementary School Journal, 90,* 193–206.

Spring, J. H. (1975). *A primer of libertarian education.* New York: Free Life Editions.

Sullivan, E. (1984). *A critical psychology.* New York: Plenum Press.

U.S. Department of Education. (1986). *What works: Research about teaching and learning.* Washington, DC: Author.

U.S. Departments of Labor and Education. (1988). *The bottom line: Basic skills in the workplace.* Washington, DC: Office of Public Information.

Wallace, T., & Walberg, H. J. (1991). Parental partnerships for learning. *International Journal of Educational Research, 15,* 131–145.

Walmsley, S. A. (1981). On the purpose and content of secondary reading programs: An educational ideological perspective. *Curriculum Inquiry, 11,* 73–93.

8

The National Reading Research Center

Donna E. Alvermann
University of Georgia

John T. Guthrie
University of Maryland College Park

This chapter consists of our collective reactions to the six chapters that precede it, a description of the National Reading Research Center (NRRC)—its mission, people, research programs, collaborations, forthcoming products, publications, and activities—and an analysis of how the NRRC reflects or transcends the projections described in the previous chapters. Although we write as co-directors of the NRRC, we wish to acknowledge the thinking of our university- and school-based colleagues, who in their roles as principal investigators contributed substantively to the design of the NRRC. In the end, of course, we take full responsibility for any omissions or imperfections in our writing.

COLLECTIVE REACTIONS TO PRECEDING CHAPTERS

The authors of the six chapters represent a broad spectrum of views on reading research and instruction, and they speak from both the researcher's and practitioner's perspectives. Yet in spite of their diversity, they are remarkably united in several of their projections for Reading Research into the Year 2000. For example, each author acknowledged the importance of investigating the social contexts of literacy instruction, the nature of children's development in learning to read and write, the inequities in reading achievement, and the research/practice relationship. Although research on technology and learning subject matter from texts and other curricular materials received less attention, these two areas are included in the discussion that follows because they form a major part of four of the six authors' research projections in the preceding chapters.

Social Contexts of Literacy Instruction

Generally, there is agreement that potentially useful research exists to explain the dynamic nature of cognitively based models of literacy instruction. Instructional research has documented that many cognitive strategies (e.g., predicting, drawing inferences, and summarizing) can be taught explicitly, but it shed little light on how these strategies can be incorporated systematically into classroom routines. Children who possess the appropriate cognitive strategies for comprehending what they read may not use them in actual classroom situations. Why? Lack of motivation? Little or no interest in reading? Inability to transfer strategic knowledge?

In their search for answers to this multifaceted question, researchers are beginning to look beyond the unidimensional models of readers' internal processes, which are unaffected by real world constraints. They are finding that all cognitive acts, including reading, take place within a social and cultural context, and that this larger context can either support or impede students' progress in reading.

Citing the work of Brown, Collins, and Duguid (1989), Beck (this volume) points out that "classroom practices have been criticized specifically for decontextualizing knowledge and skills, stripping them of the cultural and physical supports of the disciplinary practices in which they are actually used" (pp. 134-135). Anderson (this volume) calls for "studies [that] examine the social contexts of early literacy" (p. 51), whereas Sulzby and others (also this volume) note the need to study individual differences across age groups in socially, linguistically, and culturally diverse settings. Clearly, researchers are beginning to view cognitive acts in reading and reading instruction as being socially situated. Questions about the extent to which different social contexts mediate reading and writing instruction at all grade levels remain unanswered.

Developmental Nature of Reading and Writing

To understand fully how children learn to read and write, researchers generally agree on the need to study that process from preschool onward through the secondary school years. The authors of the six chapters in this book view the prekindergarten through 12th grade life span as an appropriate time for exploring children's emergent literacy abilities, their interaction with adults in intergenerational and home literacy activities, and their transition from emergent to conventional readers and writers. However, there was some disagreement among the chapter authors as to where the emphasis should be placed in studying the development of literate behavior.

For example, Beck and Anderson (this volume) would emphasize study-ing, among other things, the impact of whole language approaches and phonemic awareness on children's acquisition of reading. Taking a more global perspective, Sulzby (this volume) would place emphases on study-ing "when literacy begins and what counts as literacy" (p. 85). For Mosenthal and Scroggins (this volume), the emphasis would be on con-ducting research that takes into account the need for equality of learning opportunities for all students regardless of race, ethnic, or socioeconomic backgrounds. And for Monahan, who believes that there is presently too little emphasis on middle and secondary school literacy development, the need would be for research on how to motivate students to become strategic readers, or readers capable of integrating reading, writing, speaking, and listening across the content areas.

Regardless of their differences, the six authors generally agreed that investigating how students learn to read and write in this decade is certain to offer new challenges to researchers. Culturally and linguistically diverse classrooms, social unrest, changes in the family structure, and tensions within the research community itself are but a few of the factors that will influence how studies are planned, conducted, analyzed, and reported.

Inequities in Reading Achievement

It is a well-documented problem that too many Americans lack essential reading skills (Kirsch & Jungeblut, 1986; National Commission on Excel-lence in Education, 1983). Similarly, there is consensus among scholars whose work appeals to a broad spectrum of political views that as a nation we are less literate than we could or should be (Langer, Applebee, Mullis, & Foertsch, 1990; Ravitch, 1985). In looking for reasons behind such ineq-uities in reading achievement, researchers in the past may have been too quick to point to problems with language, experiential background, and differences in school and family values. According to Scroggins (this vol-ume), in the future it may be advantageous to examine closely the assumed reasons for low reading achievement so that, if previous assumptions no longer hold, they can be replaced with new understandings. This process, over time, could conceivably lead to more equitable achievement for all.

Scroggins is not alone in recommending that researchers turn their attention toward those students who are struggling to become literate. The other authors also addressed the need to study long-term and theoretically based instructional interventions, such as Reading Recovery (Deford, Lyons, & Pinnell, 1991) and Reciprocal Teaching (Palincsar & Brown, 1984). Unlike her co-contributors, however, Scroggins focused on the needs of inner-city children. She stressed the importance of developing and assess-ing the effectiveness of literacy materials that fit urban lifestyles, that challenge and enrich every child's learning, and that represent the literature of African Americans, Hispanics, Native Americans, and Asians. Scroggins also called for research on parent involvement in the education of urban children.

Research/Practice Relationship

As we read this volume's six chapters to obtain a collective sense of the projections being made for Reading Research into the Year 2000, we were struck by the numerous references to the need for collaborative efforts between university- and school-based researchers. Our own experiences in working collaboratively to build sound relationships with school-based researchers told us this was an important need. We were pleased, therefore, to see the emphasis our co-contributors placed on the research/practice relationship.

In the past, according to Mosenthal (this volume), reading researchers have tended to leave practitioners out of the agenda setting process and designed their studies around theoretical concerns rather than actual classroom situations. The assumption has been that practitioners can be convinced "that their problems and goals are similar (if not identical) to the problems and goals...investigated by reading researchers" (p. 229). As a result of this center-to-periphery approach to agenda setting, Mosenthal argued that "researchers have ignored the real problems and goals that they are purportedly entrusted to solve and facilitate" (p. 232). Approaching research in this fashion also has social and political connotations. For example, Mosenthal noted that because most of the reading research conducted in the past was done by middle-class White researchers and focused largely on similar types of readers, the goals and problems of readers in minority classes were all but neglected.

Generally, the perception of Mosenthal's co-contributors is that reading research has made a difference in classroom practice. For example, Anderson noted the influence of concepts like *story grammar, schema, phonemic awareness,* and *automaticity* on reading education. Beck pointed out that teachers no longer view reading as a process for getting meaning from the printed page, but rather, as an interactive process in which readers construct meaning based on information in the text and from their own experiences.

Monahan and Scroggins also acknowledged the abundance of research recommendations for practitioners; however, speaking as practitioners, they are deeply concerned about the need for greater implementation of what is already known. Monahan suggested one way to solve the implementation problem is to involve teachers as researchers who investigate their own classroom practices and then act on what they find. Interestingly, this suggestion falls squarely within the argument that Mosenthal made when he called for the involvement of practitioners in setting reading research agendas.

Technology

Broadened definitions of literacy, or multiple literacies as some individuals have described the phenomenon, remind us that we live in a rapidly changing world where limited access to traditional texts does not necessarily equate with limited access to the information presented in those texts. As Sulzby (this volume) points out, in even the most print-impoverished homes, children are likely to have access to videotapes, computer games, and home videodisc players. Yet, she goes on to note, "[researchers] have tended to ignore software development or treat it as atheoretical...[despite its] great power to define the literacies that children experience" (p. 118).

Technology's ability to capture the imagination of readers and writers has not been fully explored, particularly in terms of its potential for changing students' social interaction patterns and their response to literature. Nor is there sufficient research on how textual information might be presented and learned differently in electronic and printed forms.

Clearly, the teacher is a key determiner of how effectively computers are used to enhance a classroom's literacy curriculum and who has access to them. Teachers who have little interest in computer-based instruction may find reasons for ignoring the medium completely, unless, as Monahan suggested, they are encouraged to participate in professional development seminars that actively involve them in the medium. Promising avenues of research on the uses of technology in the classroom, according to Monahan, should focus on developing or refining strategies that highlight the teacher-as-thinker model of instruction.

Learning Subject Matter from Texts
and Other Materials

The ability to learn from subject matter texts and other printed materials is a mark of one's independence as a literate person. It is also an indication that one is able to think critically and draw reasonable conclusions about the information presented. At no time in our history has the need for critical readers been greater; yet, as Anderson (this volume) points out, "evidence continues to appear that U. S. students do not reason well about written material" (p. 65). In attempting to identify the forces that may be conspiring against students' attainment of higher order literacy, Anderson considers several possibilities, the most basic of which is that "there simply are not well-worked out and widely recognized instructional strategies for promoting critical thinking within the field of reading" (p. 67). Like Beck, he places a high priority on research that has the potential to develop students' ability to read and think critically about extended and multiple-text presentations.

We suspect that a dearth of appropriate and well-known instructional strategies for fostering critical thinking is not the only force conspiring against students' success in learning from subject matter texts. Motivation to read complex prose written in expository style about topics that have little or no relevance for their everyday lives must surely be low for most students. Beck (this volume) recognizes the problem of low motivation when she recommends that researchers "continue both cognitive and motivational work on developing techniques to encourage students' active engagement with text" (p. 165). Similarly, Monahan's recommendation that researchers concentrate on helping middle and secondary school readers develop strategies for coping with conceptually dense texts is another indication that students' motivation for learning from subject matter texts needs bolstering.

Summary

Based on our readings of the six chapters in this book, we feel confident that the NRRC's agenda has both the depth and breadth needed to address the issues and recommendations made by the chapter authors. However, as we indicated earlier, our plan is first to describe the NRRC and then to analyze how we believe it either reflects or transcends our co-contributors' projections for *Reading Research into the Year 2000*.

THE NRRC'S MISSION

One of the national goals proposed for American education by former President Bush was that by the year 2000, every adult American will be literate, possess the skills to compete in a global economy, and be prepared to exercise the rights and responsibilities of citizenship. To achieve this goal of nationwide literacy, the NRRC must acknowledge and address four pervasive problems.

First and foremost is the well-documented problem that too many Americans lack the ability and desire to read and write. An astonishing proportion of students and youth lack the broad range of literacy skills needed for their own learning and productive participation in society (SCANS, 1991). Too many students who can read choose to avoid the printed word, even at their own peril (Foertsch, 1992). We address this problem by carrying out research that fosters readers' critical thinking and strategic learning, promotes their engagement in literacy activities, and prepares them to meet the challenges of a technological age.

A second problem is the crisis in equity. It is time to acknowledge and confront the persistent lack of equity in the reading achievement of mainstream and non-mainstream students in the United States. Clearly, we are failing to meet the literacy needs of today's socially and culturally diverse student population. To alter this situation, we will conduct research that explores sociocultural issues in literacy achievement and how best to address them in classrooms, homes, and communities across the country.

A third problem is the nature of current reading instruction. Although there have been significant advances in the last two decades in our understanding of the reading process and how to teach reading, this understanding has not had a widespread impact on classroom practice (Alvermann & Moore, 1991; Wendler, Samuels, & Moore, 1989). With few exceptions, reading instruction today looks remarkably similar to that of the 1950s, with a basal reader program, three ability-level groups, a student workbook, and an end-of-the-year standardized test. Why is this the case? We believe that, despite efforts to disseminate research on reading instruction, the findings have not addressed teachers' questions dealing with the complexities of teaching students to read and respond in actual classrooms. Consequently, we will involve teachers as full participants in research, and we will establish permanent research sites in the schools.

The fourth problem is the prevalence of decontextualized reading research. We know a great deal about how typical readers process information in carefully controlled situations but relatively little about how they construct meaning in the contexts in which they are usually required to read. Moreover, we now have evidence that the cognitive act of reading is influenced by social and motivational factors (Brown, Collins, & Duguid, 1989), which can either facilitate or impede students' attempts to construct meaning from text. These two facts suggested to us the need for a reality check on what teachers currently view as worthy of research. Not wishing to perpetuate the study of reading in artificially contrived settings or for purposes that have little chance of helping students, we conducted a national poll of teachers in which we asked respondents to identify and rank problems warranting research. The results of the poll (O'Flahavan et al., 1992) indicated that teachers' number one priority is finding ways to motivate and create an interest in reading. This finding led directly to what we have come to call an engagement perspective for our research.

Engagement Perspective

Working within an engagement perspective, our overarching goal is to study how to cultivate highly engaged, self-determining readers who are the architects of their own learning. A unifying theme running throughout our research is that students will acquire the competencies and motivations to read for diverse aesthetic and academic purposes, such as gaining knowledge, interpreting an author's perspective, escaping into the literary world, performing a task, sharing reactions to stories and informational texts, or taking social and political action in response to what is read. In short, highly engaged readers are motivated, knowledgeable, strategic, and socially interactive.

Research has documented that a reader's engagement with texts is a strong predictor of her or his success in reading (Morrow & Weinstein, 1986). Likewise, considerable support for an engagement perspective was drawn from the evidence that children play a role in their own educational development by the choices they make about how to spend their time (Scarr & McCartney, 1983).

An engagement perspective, which is congruent with highly respected views on reading acquisition and instruction, recognizes the social nature of cognition. This perspective is useful for addressing the four problems that currently stand as roadblocks to achieving nationwide literacy by the year 2000, as outlined in our mission statement. It is also a useful heuristic for ensuring that the NRRC's research agenda is coherent and capable of taking into account the multiple and intersecting needs of students, parents, policymakers, and teachers. According to a recent publication by the National Academy of Education (1991), "the interests of students, institutions and society as a whole may be better served by discovering more productive forms of engagement with learning" (p. 39).

Research Objectives

Guided by an engagement perspective, researchers at the National Reading Research Center will pursue the following objectives:

- Describe the growth of students' motivation to read at home and in school.
- Extend the knowledge base on the cognitive processes of reading by relating these processes to social and motivational dimensions of instruction.
- Chronicle the effects of long-term strategy instruction on the motivational and cognitive development of students of diverse cultures and abilities.
- Describe and develop social, cognitive, and language bridges from home to school for emergent readers.
- Explore how schools appropriate technology to enhance literacy and increase the amount and diversity of students' independent reading.
- Study the influences that innovative social participation patterns have on literary interpretation, higher order thinking during content area reading, and sustained motivation for sharing books.
- Examine and design new literature-based curricula and instruction for first and second grade learners, emphasizing programs for students who are placed at-risk for reading failure.
- Trace knowledge acquisition during reading in science, math, geography, and history classes in collaboration with content teachers in these areas.
- Evaluate alternative reading assessments, establish standards for teacher-based assessments, and develop policy-based alternative assessments.

- Affirm our commitment to collaborative research, which enables us to define and describe teacher development in teacher-researcher communities, preservice education, and local school system initiatives.

In summary, our vision for the NRRC is based on the belief that there should be a dynamic, reciprocal relationship between theory and practice—that theory can inform practice and practice can enlighten theory. Therefore, NRRC activities will enlist teachers as collaborative researchers and establish permanent research sites where university- and school-based researchers plan, conduct, synthesize and report research. When teachers engage in research, posing problems and examining their own work, there is inherently a bridge between theory and practice. Teacher inquiry develops ownership of the research questions, enhances the credibility of the findings, and fosters dissemination.

PEOPLE IN THE NRRC

Diversity in scholarship requires a diverse set of human resources. The NRRC is fortunate to have both. The principal investigators comprise a representative cross-section of the research interests and methodologies necessary for moving literacy research forward into the year 2000. There is a strong commitment to cultural diversity, teacher involvement, and broad geographic representation.

Principal Investigators

In the first two years of the grant, the NRRC has a total of 71 investigators working on 41 different projects. In addition to their research expertise, the university-based researchers have a strong record of involvement with the public schools and educational agencies. They were involved in a significant number of highly successful collaborations with classroom teachers in the past, an important characteristic given the NRRC's emphasis on school-based teacher research (see the following section on teacher involvement).

The university-based researchers represent an array of disciplines and hail from colleges of education, child and family development, and arts and sciences. The majority of these researchers have their doctorates in reading education, psychology, educational psychology, elementary education, English/language arts education, and curriculum and instruction. Most have been involved previously in long-term externally funded research projects and bring a wealth of experiences to the NRRC. Several principal investigators were Fulbright Scholars or have spent time as invited scholars at major research institutions in the United States and abroad.

Although not principal investigators themselves, the 10 members of the

NRRC's National Advisory Board complement the research interests and methodologies represented in the NRRC. For example, members of the National Advisory Board, which meets annually with principal investigators to contribute to the evolving vision of the NRRC and to review previous accomplishments, include experts in the areas of literary theory, measurement, textual analysis, sociolinguistics, multicultural education, large- and small-scale assessment, cultural anthropology, and school administration.

Cultural Diversity

We believe that the inclusion of researchers from diverse racial and ethnic backgrounds is essential to the ultimate success of the NRRC's mission. As outlined in our mission statement, one of the problems the NRRC will address is equity in reading achievement. The participation of diverse perspectives is vital to this line of inquiry. Currently, 15% of the first 2 years' projects include minority investigators. We plan to expand this number in the last 3 years of the grant, and there is a distinct possibility that more minority scholars will join projects with a Year 2 start-up date.

In addition to the principal investigators, a host of individuals agreed to collaborate in the NRRC's research. These individuals, many of whom are Hispanic, Asian, or African Americans, include classroom teachers and their students, school administrators, policymakers at the local and state level, and undergraduate as well as graduate research assistants. The NRRC is committed to recruiting graduate research assistants from colleges and universities that historically have had high percentages of minority students.

Three of the NRRC's ten National Advisory Board members are members of underserved groups. We have also established links with the University of Georgia's National Center for the Gifted and Talented whose dual mission is to identify gifted students in underserved populations and to create curricula that reflect the lives of these students.

Teacher Involvement

We are equally committed to including teachers as full participants in the design, implementation, interpretation, dissemination, and evaluation of the NRRC's research. As stated in the mission statement, two of the problems we will address include the status quo nature of current reading instruction and the prevalence of decontextualized reading research. When findings from research on literacy instruction stem from the concerns of researchers rather than teachers, there is little chance that the research will make lasting differences in classroom practice. The same holds true for research that is conducted outside of classrooms in laboratory-like settings or in artificially contrived settings within schools.

Consequently, the NRRC seeks to avoid what Mosenthal (this volume) calls the center-to-periphery approach to agenda setting, whereby researchers identify the problems they want to research without involving teachers in substantive ways. More than 30% of the NRRC's investigators are classroom teachers, district-level curriculum coordinators, administrators, or members of state boards of education. Approximately 85% of the projects are school-based and involve teachers and students working in their natural settings, whereas the remaining projects involve home, library, community center, and book club settings.

Practitioners are represented in other groups as well. Most of the NRRC's graduate research assistants have had considerable classroom teaching experience, and four of the National Advisory Board members represent practitioners in one or more of these dual capacities: as a teacher, a member of the National Assessment Governing Board, an editor of a national education journal, a project director for the National Diffusion Network, a curriculum coordinator, or a member of a state department of education.

Broad Geographic Representation

The NRRC's principal investigators are located at sites that represent a broad geographic spectrum. Six of the 41 projects are at sites other than the University of Georgia and the University of Maryland. These are called Affiliated Scholar Projects and are located at the University of Washington in Seattle, San Diego State University in southern California, the University of Texas at Austin, Clark Atlanta University in Atlanta, Georgia, the University of Virginia in Charlottesville, and Rutgers University in New Jersey. Broad geographic representation adds to the richness of the NRRC's diverse population and makes possible some measure of cross-fertilization of ideas across the various sites. It also provides a diverse set of schools, communities, and homes in which to carry out the NRRC's research agenda.

RESEARCH PROGRAMS IN THE NRRC

The scope of the NRRC's research embraces the three major program areas—instruction, learning, and assessment—described in Sweet and Anderson (this volume) plus a fourth area, teacher development. The first three program areas were identified by the U.S. Department of Education's Office of Educational Research and Improvement as a result of an extensive effort to tap the various constituencies and individuals who have an interest in improving literacy. This included holding roundtables at major education research conferences, commissioning the six chapters included in this book, co-sponsoring an IRA panel discussion by the authors of the six chapters, and soliciting comments from the public at large through advertisements placed in highly visible publications that appeal to researcher and practitioner audiences.

We elected to add the fourth program area on teacher development because we believe that successful instruction, learning, and assessment in reading must engage teachers as well as learners. Although many of the program area projects include aspects of teacher development, they do not focus on how teachers become engaged participants in their own professional growth and how this engagement influences their beliefs, knowledge, and actions. Research that is not informed by practice stands little chance of changing practice, especially when teachers' beliefs are at odds with the theories underlying the proposed changes (Richardson, Anders, Tidwell, & Lloyd, 1991). Moreover, traditional professional development activities will not change instruction if teachers' philosophical and pedagogical orientations to reading are overlooked and if teachers are not actively involved in the change process (Gitlin, 1990).

Instruction

The research projects in this program area comprise four interrelated strands of inquiry. In the first strand, *literature and early reading*, researchers are studying the sociocultural, cognitive, and motivational aspects of reading instruction for the emergent and primary grade reader. The studies in this strand focus on literature-based reading programs, holistic approaches, and the principles of Reading Recovery lessons as they apply primarily in low-income, inner-city classrooms. One of the four studies is longitudinal; it follows a cohort of students from first through third grades to determine how changes in literacy programs and literacy instruction affect students' growth in literacy. This study includes teachers in small and large school districts located in rural and urban areas that serve both high and low SES students.

In the second strand, *comprehension and cognitive strategies*, the emphasis is on year-long strategy instruction in which teachers attempt to replicate in their regular classrooms the comprehension strategies that researchers previously found effective, but under less naturalistic conditions. These studies incorporate a mix of instructional alternatives, including transactional strategy instruction, comprehension monitoring, literature discussion groups, sensory impression instruction, repeated readings, directed reading activities, and dialogical-thinking reading lessons. They examine how strategies empower students to select challenging reading and learning tasks.

Researchers in the third strand, *knowledge-rich contexts*, are focusing on content area reading instruction in science, history, and geography at the middle and secondary school level. They intend to describe how various models of concept-centered reading instruction support students' cognitive, social, and motivational development. In one of the studies, the science

teacher, reading specialist, and university-based researcher are implementing a year-long "hands-on" science curriculum in which Chapter 1 students
are taught how to generate questions about an observed phenomenon and
then search for answers using a variety of print sources (texts, trade books,
reference books, and illustrations). This study examines how students learn
to select books and materials to meet their interests and satisfy their
curiosities. Mapping the changes in children's intrinsic motivations for
reading over the year is one aim of the investigation. Year 2 of the study
will include an evaluation of the model after it has been implemented in
eight classrooms across three schools.

In the fourth strand, *social contexts of instruction*, the goal is to introduce
innovative social participation structures that can lead to higher order
thinking and sustained motivation for reading. Participation structures
include student-led and teacher-led discussions of expository texts, computer-based reading and writing activities aimed at increasing the amount
and diversity of students' independent reading, and cross-age peer tutoring. The studies embrace a cross-section of K–12 rural, suburban, and
urban classrooms with student populations ranging from low to high in
socioeconomic and cultural diversity. In one of the studies, university
student athletes who are experiencing difficulty in reading will tutor elementary students who have been placed at-risk for reading failure. The goal
is to determine whether a tutoring program that includes instruction in
phonemic awareness, story writing, and the reading of children's literature
will improve the reading skills and attitudes of both the tutors and the
children they tutored.

Learning

The research projects in this program area cluster into three strands: emergent literacy and language development, motivation for reading, and learning from text. Each of these strands is supported by the engagement
perspective, with a fundamental assumption that learning to read and
write, as well as learning *from* reading and writing, depend critically on
having ready access to print-rich environments. In the first strand, *emergent
literacy and language development*, that access can be through the home,
school, or community. However, not all students have equal access to
print-rich environments, as the studies in this strand will demonstrate. For
example, a 4-year longitudinal study will follow students coming from
low-income African-American families, low-income White families, and
middle-income White families as they move from pre-kindergarten
through second grade. In doing so, the study will allow for a more complete
specification of the variety of contexts and processes contributing to the
development of literacy than is presently available. In another longitudinal
study involving low-income families, two school-based researchers will
describe how three-way dialogue journals involving themselves, their

students, and their students' parents affected the family/school relationship and the students' literacy development.

One clear message from the Maryland–Georgia national poll of teachers is that research is needed on how children develop *motivation for reading,* the second strand within this program area on learning. Consequently, researchers are working from the perspective that engaged readers use sophisticated reading strategies in accordance with their motivations for doing so. Discovering what those uniquely personal motivations are and how to channel them for improved learning is the goal of several of the studies in this strand. For example, a 5-year longitudinal study involving 7th- and 8th-grade students as co-researchers will follow these students through high school for the purpose of examining conditions that support or impede students' continuing impulse to learn and respond. Another study will investigate why librarians traditionally have been left out of the dialogue on literacy and learning, a curious fact given that access to libraries is known to have a positive effect on children who come from print-impoverished environments (Guthrie & Greaney, 1991).

The last strand, *learning subject matter from text,* explores the importance of providing students with ready access to print-rich environments, particularly within middle and secondary school content area classrooms. Some types of texts have specific characteristics that require students to use specialized strategies if they are to learn from them. The story problem in middle school mathematics classes is one such text type. Other texts students are required to read include multiple documents on the same topic (as in history classes), computer-presented texts, and texts varying widely in quality and accuracy. Researchers in this strand look at each of these types of texts and the effects they have on students' learning. For example, one researcher is examining multicultural literature using a typology of ethnic identity to see what effects positive and negative depictions of various ethnic groups have on students' engagement in learning from this literature.

Assessment

The distinguishing characteristic of the research in this program area is its emphasis on studying assessment from the perspective of the test user, not the test developer. The focus is on investigating how alternative performance-based reading assessments compare to traditional standardized reading tests, and how they influence the instruction and learning of children who have difficulty learning to read. For example, researchers are examining portfolio assessments to determine the aspects of reading, writing, thinking, and social interaction that are likely and unlikely to be measured with these kinds of assessments.

In addressing standards for alternative assessments, one team of researchers will look at issues of design, validity, reliability, usefulness, and the ease with which results can be reported and interpreted. Another team of researchers will be observing and interviewing consumers of assessment information (e.g., teachers, parents, administrators, and the general public) both in inner-city and suburban schools to determine how this information relates to their views of students, schools, literacy instruction, and their own beliefs about achievement in reading.

A national perspective on assessment is also present. The alternative assessments that are central to the National Assessment of Educational Progress and the New Standards Project are being examined in generic form. The goals, contents, formats, and administrative contexts of these large-scale assessments are being examined in terms of their relationship to instruction in qualitative studies of schools and surveys of statewide practices. Finally, a team of researchers is conducting a national survey of research-based performance assessment tools for the purpose of constructing an annotated reference source on alternative reading assessments.

Teacher Development

Research projects described in this program area reflect the view that traditional staff development workshops typically do not produce significant and lasting changes in classroom practices because they tend to ignore teachers' philosophical and pedagogical orientations and/or they fail to involve teachers in the change process. The studies also reflect an engagement perspective on teacher development: the assumption is that instruction, learning, and assessment in literacy-related activities must engage teachers as well as learners.

Three of the six studies in this program area are longitudinal in design, with one being for a period of 5 years. The 5-year study, which is presently underway, is in partnership with the League of Professional Schools (see the next section of this chapter for a description of the league schools). Currently, this study has two of its four components in place: the elementary whole language component (in two county schools) and the community literacy program. Still to be initiated are a middle or secondary school component and a preschool education program. In working out the rationale for the elementary component, teachers in both schools established increasing students' motivation to read as their number one priority. The other two longitudinal studies will explore how teachers' beliefs and knowledge about teaching literacy change over time and how this change may influence their instructional decisions, assessments, and actions. The focus of one of these studies is a school-based teacher education program that embraces the Foxfire (Wigginton, 1986) philosophy of teaching.

A fourth research project in this area is a study of how information learned in district-level professional development courses is incorporated into teachers' instructional repertoires. The remaining two studies have a multicultural emphasis. One is designed to establish the cultural knowledge base necessary for guiding preservice teachers as they modify an existing curriculum in order to achieve a better fit with the reading attitudes and interests of inner-city African American children. The other study explores how teachers develop understandings of literacy instruction for multicultural populations by participating in book clubs where they read and discuss contemporary fiction written by authors from the same cultural background as their students.

PLANNED COLLABORATIONS AND OTHER ACTIVITIES

The NRRC is committed to collaborations and other related activities that will enable it to be informed by practice as well as to inform practice. The goal is to maintain an open and two-way communication with its various constituencies: teachers, school administrators, reading and curriculum specialists, professional organizations, policymakers, parents, and children themselves. For research to be implemented it must first be perceived as relevant to the people who will use it and benefit from it. We believe the best way to ensure such relevancy is to maintain a two-way communication between the NRRC and the outside world.

To establish this two-way communication, we have several collaborative projects and related activities already underway; others are in the planning stage and will be initiated during the second year of the grant. For ease of presentation, we have grouped these activities into three categories: school networks, professional organizations and conferences, and written and electronic communications. Following is a sampling of the activities from each of these categories.

School Networks

To facilitate the substantial amount of research that will be conducted with school-based researchers, the NRRC plans to work collaboratively with interested schools in establishing School Research Centers. This effort extends the collaborative designs that are being used in such locations as Michigan, New York, Arizona, California, and Ohio. The School Research Centers will provide a place for university- and school-based research teams to plan, implement, analyze, interpret, and report their research. They will also provide a daily, ongoing source of information from the field. Site selection criteria will be sensitive to the need for School Research Centers that reflect diversity both in the student populations served and in the teachers from those schools.

Researchers at the University of Maryland have established long and fruitful working relationships with the schools in their state and the Greater Washington, DC area. These collaborative arrangements and similar ones established with the Maryland State Department of Education have added immeasurably to the NRRC's credibility in conducting school- and community-based research. For example, a program sponsored collaboratively by the University of Maryland and several local schools operates six Teacher Education Centers, which have been recognized as exemplary by the AACTE.

At the Maryland site, teacher-researcher communities are being developed. Teachers convene with university researchers to study their own teaching and to reflect on the processes of literacy learning. Beliefs and actions about reading and instruction are reevaluated by all members of the community, leading to a heightened sense of teacher professionalism.

The NRRC is in the process of forming an active partnership with The League of Professional Schools. Currently comprised of 50 schools with 2,000 K–12 teachers, the League has been recognized for the past 2 years as one of the top 10 educational collaboratives in the United States by the National Business/Higher Education Alliance. League schools are committed to shared governance and to implementing educational practices that enhance teaching and learning opportunities for faculty and students across a wide spectrum of school structures. The league's director, Carl Glickman, is on the faculty at the University of Georgia and interested in establishing collaborative research projects with the NRRC.

A team of researchers from the NRRC has been invited to enter a dialogue on how they might become involved in The Carter Center Atlanta Project, which is former President Jimmy Carter's plan for improving conditions in inner-city schools. Currently there are 12 high schools targeted by the project where literacy is low and where dropout rates, violence, and alienation are high.

Several university-based researchers in the NRRC have close working ties with the Writing Projects Network and Teaching-as-a-Researching Profession. Both networks support long-established teacher research projects and the dissemination of findings from those projects.

Professional Organizations and Conferences

One way of reaching out to and being reached by school-based personnel is through special sessions at professional meetings and conferences. For example, we are planning to solicit input from the field through innovative forums like the "Town Meeting." This format will allow us to share information about the NRRC's mission and research in progress while simultaneously gathering information about teachers' concerns and questions. Teams of school- and university-based researchers from the NRRC will moderate the Town Meetings to keep the dialogue flowing and to share what they have learned with their colleagues back home.

Many educators belong to professional organizations that do not typically disseminate literacy research through their conferences or publications. To reach this audience, we have contacted the directors of large umbrella groups like the National Education Association to seek their interest and collaboration in disseminating research highlights and other resource materials on literacy development. Such organizations typically have powerful caucuses or special interest groups that are politically active and well-connected to various educational networks around the country.

The NRRC sponsored a national conference for February 12–13, 1993 at the University of Georgia. The conference theme was developing engaged readers through family, school, and community-based research. Teachers, researchers, and key policymakers from state and national levels were involved. A highly interactive format was planned, one in which participants had the opportunity to respond to ideas presented at the conference as well as introduce their own questions and concerns. Currently there are plans to include a teleconference segment in which people at distant sites can interact "live" with the presenters and participants in Georgia. During conferences such as this one, we expect to establish collaborative arrangements that will become part of Years 3, 4, and 5 of the grant.

Written and Electronic Communications

Prior to developing and submitting a proposal to OERI for the National Reading Research Center, we polled a stratified sample of 1,000 literacy educators, comprised mostly of classroom teachers and reading specialists, to seek their opinions on what issues and problems warranted further research. The results were used to inform our research agenda. We plan to continue this poll in order to maintain a sense of how the National Reading Research Center is meeting the needs of its constituents.

During the second year of the grant, we plan to publish an NRRC newsletter that will be available to a wide audience of educators, policymakers, and other interested parties by subscription. Plans include having the newsletter feature questions and issues taken from the NRRC's electronic networks (discussed later), regular columns by teams of NRRC university- and school-based researchers across the country, and research-based suggestions geared to teachers in elementary, middle, and secondary schools.

METNET, an electronic network maintained by the Maryland State Department of Education's Instructional Technology Branch, has an 800 telephone number that will provide free access to its electronic forum and bulletin board. Researchers, school-based personnel, and interested policymakers throughout the country can tap into this free source of information. A METNET file on the NRRC's publications, conferences, teacher resources, and videotapes will be maintained to assist network users in obtaining the latest information on literacy research.

Two other types of electronic bulletin boards will provide the communication links necessary for collaborations to occur between the NRRC and the field. One is an in-house system that links the NRRC's school- and university-based researchers at all of its sites across the country; this electronic forum is currently in operation for the majority of NRRC researchers. The NRRC plans to initiate a second electronic bulletin board that will permit anyone in the United States equipped with a microcomputer and access to one of several on-line networks (e.g., BITNET, INTERNET, ON-LINE AMERICA) to interact with NRRC personnel. An NRRC staff member will be responsible for providing an updated listing and description of the NRRC's resources. Questions directed to the NRRC will be acknowledged in several ways, including personal responses and information on how to obtain access to research findings.

FORTHCOMING PRODUCTS AND PUBLICATIONS

The NRRC's dissemination plan is geared to meet a variety of audiences for whom reading research is of vital interest. In addition to the usual technical research reports and articles, we plan to produce teacher-oriented resources and demonstration videos. These products will be advertised through the publications of various professional associations. We will also communicate directly through annual book-length syntheses of scholarly work on literacy teaching and learning, and through regularly published research highlights and policy briefs.

Technical Research Reports

Investigators will submit technical reports of their research, written in a scholarly fashion but as free from jargon as possible to make them accessible to a variety of audiences. These reports will be sent to the NRRC Publications Advisory Board, which is charged with ensuring high standards of research and writing.

Teacher-Oriented Resources

We are especially committed to putting relevant research findings into the hands of as many teachers as possible, and in formats they will find immediately useful. To do this, we plan to produce a wide array of resources to support teachers in teaching reading and in using written materials. For example, researchers at the NRRC will generate prototypes of performance assessment tasks in reading. Then, based on teacher piloting, the prototypes will be revised and published. Workshops in the use of these prototypes will be conducted at regional and national conferences.

Demonstration Videos

Several of the NRRC's researchers will produce demonstration videotapes in association with their classroom-based research projects. These tapes will depict teaching and learning situations that focus on the motivational, cognitive, and social aspects of literacy development. Videos illustrating instructional practices, social interactions, and print-rich environments that support the engaged reader will become tools for further research and practical use in classrooms and teacher development activities. These videotapes will vary in quality depending on their projected use as "stand-alones" (professionally produced tapes) to "work-in-progress" kinds of tapes.

Books

The NRRC will publish annually a book that synthesizes research on an important issue or theme. The first volume will focus on the engagement perspective of literacy teaching and learning. It will include the thinking of university- and school-based researchers at the Center as well as the ideas of nationally recognized experts in government, children's literature, and sociocultural matters.

Research Highlights

Information about the NRRC's network of professional collaborations, research findings, products, instructional materials, conferences, books, journal articles, videos, and policy briefs will be available through published research highlights. For example, the NRRC will have a regular column in *The Reading Teacher* devoted to these highlights. Plans are underway to contribute similarly to the publications of other professional organizations (e.g., *Educational Leadership*) as well as to publications read by parents (e.g., *Parents Magazine*), librarians, local school board members, and policymakers at the state and national level. In addition, the research highlights will be available through one or more of the NRRC's electronic networks.

Policy Briefs

The NRRC staff will produce policy-related research briefs and respond to questions of legislators and other decision-makers. Because those involved with public policy often prefer face-to-face dialogues, the NRRC will sponsor semiannual meetings at the University of Maryland campus.

THE NRRC: REFLECTING
AND TRANSCENDING PROJECTIONS

The essence of the NRRC's research agenda resonates nicely with our co-contributors' projections of where literacy research should be in the year 2000. In some instances it goes beyond their recommendations to include special emphasis on areas of research that the University of Georgia/University of Maryland consortium deemed important to the Center's work. Overall, we believe the NRRC research agenda incorporates exceedingly well the goals and problems of two of the three perspectives Mosenthal (this volume) identifies as crucial to making real progress in literacy research. The third perspective, what Mosenthal calls an "emancipatory perspective," is perhaps least well reflected in the NRRC's agenda, although we would submit that research aimed at exploring the goals and problems of readers from diverse cultural, socioeconomic, ethnic, and linguistic backgrounds is a prerequisite to transforming literacy practice that will be in tune with the educational needs of all Americans by the year 2000.

The National Reading Research Center's agenda builds on the work of many researchers. Because of the important contributions researchers in previous decades made in illuminating the reading process, the new NRRC is able to devote most of its research efforts to investigating the intricacies of how children in prekindergarten through high school socially construct knowledge from printed materials in a variety of home, school, and community contexts.

Finally, the NRRC's agenda reflects the many hours of collaboration, and especially the insights, contributed by our colleagues and co-researchers in schools and state departments of education throughout the United States. Without their constant influence and sometimes not so gentle reminders, we would have been less sensitive to the need for research that addresses literacy development as it is truly experienced—in the homes, classrooms, and communities students inhabit. To this group of educators and to all those who contributed to the national poll that informed our engagement perspective on reading, we pledge to work toward fulfilling the agenda that has been set out for us.

REFERENCES

Alvermann, D. E., & Moore, D. W. (1991). Secondary school reading. In R. Barr, M. L. Kamil, P. D. Pearson, & P. Mosenthal (Eds.), *Handbook of reading research* (Vol. 2, pp. 951–983). New York: Longman.

Brown, J. S., Collins, A., & Duguid, P. (1989). Situated cognition and the culture of learning. *Educational Researcher, 18,* 32–43.

Deford, D. E., Lyons, C., & Pinnell, G. S. (1991). *Bridges to literacy: Learning from Reading Recovery.* Portsmouth, NH: Heinemann.

Foertsch, M. A. (1992, May). *Reading in and out of school: Factors influencing the literacy achievement of American students in grades 4, 8, and 12 in 1988 and 1990.* Washington, DC: National Center for Education Statistics.

Gitlin, A. (1990). Educative research, voice, and school change. *Harvard Educational Review, 60,* 443–466.

Guthrie, J. T., & Greaney, V. (1991). Literacy acts. In R. Barr, M. L. Kamil, P. D. Pearson, & R. Barr (Eds.), *Handbook of reading research* (Vol. 2, pp. 68–96). New York: Longman.

Kirsch, I., & Jungeblut, A. (1986). *Literacy: Profiles of America's young adults.* Princeton, NJ: Educational Testing Service.

Langer, J. A., Applebee, A. N., Mullis, I. V. S., & Foertsch, M. (1990). *Learning to read in our nation's schools: Instruction and achievement in 1988 at grades 4, 8, and 12.* Princeton, NJ: Educational Testing Service.

Morrow, L. M., & Weinstein, C. S. (1986). Encouraging voluntary reading: The impact of a literature program on children's use of library centers. *Reading Research Quarterly, 21,* 330–346.

National Academy of Education. (1991). *Research and the renewal of education.* New York: Carnegie Corporation.

National Commission on Excellence in Education. (1983). *A nation at risk: The imperative for educational reform.* Washington, DC: U.S. Department of Education.

O'Flahavan, J., Gambrell, L. B., Guthrie, J., Stahl, S., Baumann, J. F., & Alvermann, D. E. (1992, August/September). Poll of IRA members guides National Reading Research Center. *Reading Today.*

Palincsar, A. S., & Brown, A. L. (1984). Reciprocal teaching of comprehension-fostering and monitoring activities. *Cognition and Instruction, 1,* 117–175.

Ravitch, D. (1985). *The schools we deserve: Reflections on the educational crises of our times.* New York: Basic Books.

Richardson, V., Anders, P., Tidwell, D., & Lloyd, C. (1991). The relationship between teachers' beliefs and practices in reading comprehension instruction. *American Educational Research Journal, 28,* 559–586.

SCANS (The Secretary's Commission on Achieving Necessary Skills). (1991, June). *What work requires of schools: A SCANS report for America 2000.* Washington, DC: U.S. Department of Labor.

Scarr, S., & McCartney, K. (1983). How people make their own environments: A theory of genotype environment effects. *Child Development, 54,* 424–435.

Wendler, D., Samuels, S. J., & Moore, V. K. (1989). Comprehension instruction of award-winning teachers, teachers with master's degrees, and other teachers. *Reading Research Quarterly, 24,* 382–401.

Wigginton, E. (1986). *Sometimes a shining moment: The Foxfire experience.* Garden City, NY: Anchor/Doubleday.

About the Contributors

Donna E. Alvermann is codirector of the Office for Educational Research and Improvement (OERI)-supported National Reading Research Center (NRRC) in collaboration with the University of Maryland and Professor of Reading in the College of Education at the University of Georgia; her research focuses on the role of classroom dialogue in content reading instruction. Currently she is president of the National Reading Conference and was president of the Organization of Teacher Educators in Reading and the Georgia Educational Research Association.

Judith I. Anderson is the senior program manager for the Office of Research, Office for Educational Research and Improvement (OERI); her work encompasses program management and research and development planning across substantive education research areas that reside in the four divisions within OERI's Office of Research.

Richard C. Anderson is director of the Center for the Study of Reading and professor of education and psychology at the University of Illinois. Anderson's current research interests are microanalysis of classroom reading instruction, vocabulary growth and development, and children's independent reading. He has been president of the American Educational Research Association and was chairman of the National Academy of Education—National Institute of Education Commission on Reading.

Isabel L. Beck is professor of education in the School of Education and senior scientist at the Learning Research and Development Center at the University of Pittsburgh. Beck's research interests have focused on the acquisition of reading skills, learning from text, and the development of tactics for enhancing students' abilities to learn from difficult texts. In 1988 she received the Oscar O. Causey award for outstanding reading research from the National Reading Conference.

John T. Guthrie is codirector of the Office for Educational Research and Improvement (OERI)-supported National Reading Research Center (NRRC) in collaboration with the University of Georgia and Professor of Human Development at the University of Maryland, College Park. Guthrie's current interests are understanding children's reading choices, and cognitive strategies in conceptual learning domains. At present, he is studying instruction and assessment that fosters the development of children's ability and motivation to search, comprehend, and synthesize ideas from multiple resources.

Joy N. Monahan is a district-wide reading consultant with the Orange County Public Schools in Orlando, Florida. She has a master's degree in reading from Rollins College. During her 25 years in education, she has taught kindergarten and first grade and has directed reading labs at elementary and junior- and senior-high levels. As a consultant, facilitator, and staff developer in the public schools, she developed a Content Area Reading-Learning Strategies Program that emphasizes the cognitive processes that affect reading, thinking, learning, and remembering.

Peter B. Mosenthal is professor and chair of the Reading and Language Arts Center and Director of the Reading and Language Writing Consultation Center at Syracuse University, Syracuse, New York. His research and work interests include testing and large-scale assessment; computer adaptive instruction; comprehension in the content areas; research design and methodology; defining progress in educational research, practice, and policy; and literacy in the workplace.

Sara I. Scroggins, a consultant to the Saturday Academy Bridge Program at the University of Missouri at St. Louis, is an independent literacy consultant. Her professional career spans 38 years in the St. Louis public schools as an elementary teacher, remedial reading teacher, reading clinic coordinator, and administrator in a preschool and kindergarten center.

Elizabeth Sulzby is professor of education and faculty associate in linguistics at the University of Michigan, where she is affiliated with the Center for Research in Learning and Schooling and the Combined Program in Education and Psychology. Her research area is emergent literacy and she edited, with William H. Teale, *Emergent literacy: Writing and reading*.

Anne P. Sweet is senior research associate and director for the Learning and Instruction Division, Office of Research, Office for Educational Research and Improvement (OERI); her professional experiences span national, state, and local levels, and include positions in higher education, public school teaching, and school district leadership (director of instruction & testing, and associate superintendent).

Author Index

Subject Index